MISSION
REJECTED

MISSION REJECTED

The Soldiers
Who Say
NO to Iraq

Peter Laufer

JOHN BLAKE

Published by John Blake Publishing Ltd,
3 Bramber Court, 2 Bramber Road,
London W14 9PB, UK
www.blake.co.uk

First published in Great Britain in paperback in 2007

First published in 2006 by Chelsea Green Publishing Company,
PO Box 428, White River Junction, VT 05001, USA.

ISBN: 978-1-84454-363-2

British Library Cataloguing-in-Publication Data:
A catalogue record for this book is available from the British
Library.

Design by www.envydesign.co.uk

Printed in Great Britain by CPD, Wales.

1 3 5 7 9 10 8 6 4 2

Papers used by John Blake Publishing are natural, recyclable
products made from wood grown in sustainable forests.
The manufacturing processes conform to the environmental
regulations of the country of origin.

For Sheila, with love and gratitude

CONTENTS

FOREWORD

by Clare Short MP

It is now widely accepted that the invasion of Iraq has been a disaster and that "if the situation in Iraq continues to deteriorate, the consequences could be severe for Iraq, the United States, the region and the world." This view is no longer confined to critics of the war, but is the unanimous conclusion of the Iraq Study Group published on 6 December 2006. This is a ten member bipartisan panel appointed in March 2006 by the United States Congress, that was charged with assessing the situation in Iraq and the U.S.-led Iraq war and making policy recommendations. It is also the publicly stated view of the newly appointed Chief of the U.K. General Staff, General Sir Richard Dannatt, who said in a newspaper interview in October 2006 that we should "get ourselves out sometime soon because our presence exacerbates the security problems".

And on 19 December 2006 Britain's most respected foreign policy think tank, Chatham House, issued a report which found that Britain's decision to back the U.S. war in Iraq was a "terrible mistake".

The general public in the U.S., the U.K. and Iraq have reached the same conclusion. According to the Iraq Study Group, 66 per cent of Americans disapprove of their government's handling of the war and 70 per cent of Iraqis have a mostly negative view of the influence of the United States on their country. 61 per cent of Iraqis approve of attacks on U.S.-led forces. According to a CNN poll conducted by Opinion Research Corporation between 15-17 December 2006, 70 per cent disapprove of the way George W. Bush is handling the situation in Iraq and 67 per cent oppose the war. A Guardian/ICM poll in the U.K. on 24 October showed that a majority of voters want British troops to be pulled out of Iraq by the end of the year. And according to an ICM poll conducted in a number of countries in early November 2006, British voters see George Bush as a greater threat to world peace than either North Korea's Kim Jong-il or Iranian President Muhammed Ahmadinejad. Only 7 per cent of British people think that military action in Iraq and Afghanistan has increased world security and only 44 per cent support the decision to go to war in Iraq.

The purpose of this book is not to rehearse these arguments. There are many books that do that and which also expose the extent of the deceit used by Bush and Blair to persuade their countries into this war. Instead, this book focuses on the individual soldiers who are forced to kill and die to prop up this failing policy. A British army officer dressed in plain clothes stopped me in Whitehall some months ago to support my criticism of Tony Blair's Iraq policy. He added that it was a terrible part of the responsibility of army officers to have to talk with the parents of those who had died under their command. He said that this was obviously always a terrible responsibility, but that when one was involved in a war in which the country did not believe and where deceit had been used to justify the war, the task was unbearable. And there has been a terribly large amount of killing and dying in Iraq. Up to December 2006 nearly 2,900 Americans have lost their lives. Another 21,000 have been wounded, many severely. 126 British service personnel have lost their lives and an estimated 1000 have been severely injured.

According to a study conducted by the Johns Hopkins University Bloomberg School of Public Health in October 2006, as many as 654,965 more Iraqis may have died since hostilities began in Iraq in March 2003 than would have been expected to under pre-war conditions. 91.8 per cent of these deaths were caused by violence and 26 per cent of them by coalition forces.

There has been much passionate public debate in the U.K. about the war and the failure to hold politicians to account. There has been a dignified campaign run by Military Families Against the War, led by parents who have lost children and feel deeply aggrieved that there is no honour in the war in which their children died. Those who support the war make constant tributes to the courage of the troops and send repeated messages of condolence to families who have lost a child. But we have heard very little from the troops themselves and in particular from soldiers who have decided that the war is wrong and have the courage to refuse to serve. This is the voice we hear in this book. It tells how low income young people are recruited with false promises into the U.S. military. And we also hear the words of those who served and can bear it no longer, who flee to Canada or go on the run. These are brave and honest young men. It takes more courage to say no than to go along with the crowd. They have not been listened to enough because unlike during much of the Vietnam War, the U.S. army is not conscripted and recruitment is therefore confined to young people with limited life opportunities whose families are not well connected and able to articulate their views through the media. The book tells the stories of a small group of people, but once you have read it you are reminded of how brutal and ugly war is for all who are involved. The politicians tell lies and make misjudgements and put at risk the lives, wellbeing and mental health of vast numbers of other people's children. In this book we hear from those soldiers who are brave enough to say no.

Clare Short MP
January 2007

PREFACE

Richard Keene, a Marylander, may have been the first American war resister. The year was 1658 when Keene refused demands from the colonial government that he be trained as a soldier in the Maryland militia. For his defiance, Keene was fined six pounds and fifteen shillings by one Sheriff Coarsey. Their encounter was brief. With his unsheathed cutlass poised for attack in one hand, Sheriff Coarsey used his free hand to hit citizen Keene while insulting him and threatening him with death. "You dog!" spat out the frustrated sheriff. "I could find it in my heart to split your brains!" [1]

The sheriff's fury notwithstanding, refusing military service was the well-respected practice of some of America's founding fathers. They or their parents had risked their lives crossing the Atlantic to escape oppression in Europe. William Penn, for example, the founder of the state named after him, was a pacifist. The concept of rejecting war was so legitimate at the time that George Washington's call to arms included a critical exemption: "All young men of suitable age [are] to be drafted," he announced, "except those with conscientious scruples against war." [2] In World War II – the so-called Good War – more than forty thousand men responded to their conscription orders by refusing military service, instead spending the war years as loyal American conscientious objectors. The Vietnam War produced some 170,000 conscientious objectors.

Soon after the U.S. invasion of Iraq in 2003, the Vietnam War–era battle cry "Hell no! We won't go!" was heard again, this time from a growing number of U.S. soldiers who had voluntarily enlisted in the military. Other soldiers were returning home shocked by what they saw and did in Iraq and vehemently opposed to the war. Rather than engage in a battle they didn't believe in, some of these volunteer soldiers filed for conscientious objector status. Others accepted harsh punishment – including prison sentences at hard labor – for refusing orders. Some went AWOL (absent without leave), while others deserted the military and fled to Canada.

This new generation of American war resisters includes professional soldiers such as twenty-four-year-old U.S. Army Private Dan Felushko. "I didn't want 'Died deluded in Iraq' over my gravestone," explained Felushko about his flight to Canada as a deserter from the war. "I saw it as wrong. If I died there or killed somebody there, that would have been more wrong." [3] Specialist Jeremy Hinzman is another American solider who chose Canada over his military career. When queried about his obligation to follow orders, his answer came fast: "I was told in basic training that if I'm given an illegal or immoral order, it is my duty to disobey it. I feel that invading and occupying Iraq is an illegal and immoral thing to do." [4]

The drama of these human stories is intense, the pain deep and palpable. "I don't know how many innocents I killed with my mortar rounds," mourned Hart Viges from his apartment in Austin, Texas. "I have my imagination to pick at for that one." Viges fought in Iraq as a member of the elite 82nd Airborne Division, then came home and underwent a powerful epiphany: "You can't wash your hands when they're covered with blood." He applied for conscientious objector status. "I'm a Christian, what was I doing holding a gun to another human being? Love thy neighbor. Pray for those who persecute you, don't shoot them."[5]

These are men and women who cannot be written off as political troublemakers or emotional misfits or cowards. Many are, in fact, heroes, individuals with the remarkable strength of character required to reject propaganda and extraordinary peer pressure, to recognize their own personal change and spiritual growth. They made a huge decision not to fight in Iraq. Or they served in the "sandbox" – GI jargon for the Middle East – only to return home disgusted and appalled by their experience and what it did to them. "Behind these bars I sit a free man because I listened to a higher power, the voice of my conscience," wrote former Army Sergeant Camilo Mejía from the prison where he was locked up for refusing to return to Iraq.[6]

It's impossible to tally just how many of the soldiers sent to fight in Iraq oppose the war. Applications for conscientious objector (CO) status, according to official figures, add up to only a few score, which is understandable; in the all-volunteer force, a soldier seeking a CO discharge must somehow prove to the military that he or she experienced a profound personal philosophical change after enlisting. Only a handful of soldiers had sought refugee status in Canada by the end of 2005, but their lawyer was convinced many more were living underground north of the U.S. border.

The Pentagon acknowledges that more than six thousand soldiers have deserted from the armed forces since the invasion of Iraq (as of early 2006),[7] but no one knows how many of them went AWOL for antiwar reasons. "I know other people are feeling the same way I am," said sailor Pablo Paredes, who publicly refused to board his Iraq-bound U.S. Navy transport ship, "and I'm hoping more people will stand up. They can't throw us all in jail."[8] Paredes was sentenced to three months of hard labor.

What is clear from my research is that many soldiers fighting in Iraq opposed – or at least questioned – the mission there, especially after they arrived in the war theater and were forced by orders and circumstances into situations that defied logic, training, and their fundamental morality. And by the end of 2005, the growing membership of Iraq War veterans in antiwar organizations showed that plenty of soldiers were returning from the Middle East horrified and disgusted with the war.

It's important, as the years pass, not to forget how the United States ended up invading and occupying Iraq. The nation was still reeling in the aftermath of the September 11, 2001, attacks on the World Trade

Center and the Pentagon. The White House was fueling fear and paranoia with its repeated warnings that those responsible for the attacks were on the verge of launching more and that the very survival of the nation was at stake. Mired in Afghanistan after overthrowing the Taliban, U.S. forces were unable to find President George W. Bush's stated nemesis, Osama bin Laden. (Remember Bush's tough Texas "We'll smoke 'em out!" talk?) Taking advantage of the free hand Congress still offered, the Bush team publicly targeted Iraq, insisting it was a looming and immediate threat.

Successfully forcing attention away from their failing campaign in Afghanistan, yet facing extraordinary opposition worldwide, they intimidated Congress into supporting a radically changed U.S. foreign policy: preemptive military action. Citing Central Intelligence Agency reports that turned out to be both misleading and false, the Bush administration painted Iraq as a rogue state threatening the Free World. The term "weapons of mass destruction" became common currency as the administration prepared for war and kept up its relentless public relations campaign. Saddam Hussein was on the verge of deploying chemical weapons, it insisted, and developing doomsday germ warfare and building nuclear bombs. Condoleezza Rice, then the national security advisor, and Vice President Dick Cheney famously employed the image of a mushroom cloud over America, courtesy of Iraq. CIA director George Tenet called his agency's intelligence "a slam-dunk" for war. Vice President Cheney publicly daydreamed about the World War II–like greeting U.S. "liberators" would enjoy from Iraqis after overthrowing Saddam Hussein. At the same time, they worked hard to stitch together another claim that soon proved false: that a direct working relationship existed between the religious fanatics of Osama bin Laden's al-Qaeda and the secular warriors of Saddam Hussein's Baath Party.

Predicated on this curriculum of deceit, the United States sent its voluntary army on another failed overseas adventure even while the memory of the Vietnam debacle was so fresh that some soldiers who had served in the Vietnam War were still young enough to be shipped off to its desert cousin in Iraq. When no weapons of mass destruction were found in Iraq, and when no valid link could be shown between Saddam Hussein and Osama bin Laden, further excuses were offered by the White House to rationalize the ongoing war: first, a U.S. obligation to bring democracy to Iraq and prevent civil war, and then, perhaps most shameful of all, to honor the soldiers already killed.

Throughout this book I refer to those in the military generically as "soldiers." Unless it is germane to their stories to specify their rank and branch of service, I find it more appropriate to think of these men and women as individuals within a monolithic military. Soldiers.

I am pleased to report that no pseudonyms are used in the book, nor are there anonymous sources among my interviewees. The soldiers telling me their stories are on the record. Only Daniel (chapter 7) kept his last name to himself, worried that his candid remarks would jeopardize his desperate attempts to regain his veteran's medical benefits as he suffered from the debilitating effects of combat-induced post-traumatic stress disorder. These are all real people laboring with some of life's most difficult decisions, all now out in the open. One after another they told me that they were motivated to share their stories, at least in part, by their desire to help other soldiers deal with similar predicaments. Many said they hoped news of their experiences would steer vulnerable civilians away from the military. And plenty of them thanked me for listening to them, telling me that speaking publicly is part of their personal healing process.

Some might question the veracity of their stories, but it is worth keeping in mind that these soldiers have no reason to lie about events that often portray them in a grotesquely negative light. Curious too, isn't it, that so many of them – separated from each other by geography and time – experienced such similar tragedies?

Many of the scenarios described cannot be fact-checked with the traditional tools. These are events and experiences that were not necessarily witnessed by anyone approaching the role of an impartial observer. Most are not logged, recorded, or filmed. But more crucial, I think, is the fact that the backbone, heart, and soul of these stories are not so much the specifics of the events recounted, but rather the epiphanies of the soldiers who experienced them.

These are stories of coming of age, stories of religious awakening, and stories of coming to terms with morality and immorality, as well as mortality. These are stories of breakups of relationships with families and country. I've looked into these soldiers' eyes. I've listened to their voices. I've watched them cry. They may have made mistakes as they recounted events, maybe even embellishing here and there – human nature suggests that's probable. There may even be some faded or foggy memories. How can there not be? But the overriding truth is clear.

Their stories are worth listening to, because they represent a different reality – an unvarnished and unfiltered reality – from that depicted by our government and much of our media. The horrors the soldiers speak of are better known abroad – in Europe, in the Middle East, in Asia – than they are at home in the United States.

Are the Iraqis (and others) who favor violence against the U.S. troops terrorists or freedom fighters? Are some of them demented followers of a perverted version of Islam who feel no remorse about blowing themselves and others to bits? Do others feel they are protecting their country and families by trying to rout out the invaders and occupiers? Are they a resistance, or insurgents, or guerrillas? Are they crazed jihadists? Leftover Saddamists? Common opportunistic criminals? Outside agitators? Are they simply hired thugs doing the dirty work for ambitious politicians and gangsters?

The answer, undoubtedly, is all of the above. Why,

then, should these combatants be categorized as a single group? Perhaps, for practical purposes, we need a term to define diverse types collectively. The challenge is to find a term that identifies such people in a summary fashion with the least possible distortion or propagandistic baggage.

"Terrorist," the catchall word favored by the Bush administration, dates to the Reign of Terror during the French Revolution. A terrorist uses terror as a device to accomplish a goal. Terror is fear and fright and dread. One critical shortcoming of the freighted word "terrorist" is that it could just as accurately be used to describe American military personnel in Iraq. Given the U.S. tactics, from the initial threat of a "shock and awe" attack to the assaults on cities whose populations rejected the U.S. occupation, American actions could accurately be termed terrorism.

"Freedom fighter," of course, is a term completely dependent on point of view. To King George and his British soldiers, George Washington and his revolutionary army were no freedom fighters. "The resistance" often is used as a proper noun, denoting a struggle for liberation in an occupied country. It also carries a heritage that evokes romantic French Resistance fighters opposing Hitler and the Nazis. "Guerrilla" tends to conjure equally romantic images of beret-clad South Americans and others fighting against oppressive authority. English borrowed the term from the Spanish diminutive meaning simply "little war," but it has come to mean combatants in an irregular war.

"Insurgent" is perhaps the term most widely used

to identify Iraqi attackers. The word comes from the Latin *insurgere*, meaning "to rise up against," and in English it can mean one who is rising up against an authority or a government in power. But for those who question the legitimacy of the U.S. occupation of Iraq, "insurgent" may have its own emotional baggage, because it is used by the U.S. armed forces. However correct it may be as a descriptive word, it can cast an unintended negative connotation. A murderous insurgent from an American soldier's point of view may be a patriotic freedom fighter to an Iraqi who feels oppressed by the occupation.

This semantic challenge is an important one. Words and their definitions are potent; they carry extraordinary power. Who is the U.S. Army fighting in Iraq, and why? Both those questions have been answered by the Bush administration through the misuse of words. The president muddied the scene further late in 2005 when he chose to identify his foe in Iraq with the term "rejectionists."[9]

Much of the media accepted the administration's labels without challenge – as they accepted the very reason for going to war without challenge. The *New York Times*, in a spotlighted mea culpa published on May 26, 2004, apologized for some of its reporting during the run-up to the Iraq invasion, acknowledging that it had published "information that was controversial then, and seems questionable now, was insufficiently qualified or allowed to stand unchallenged. Looking back, we wish we had been more aggressive in re-examining the claims as new evidence emerged – or failed to emerge."

Other news outlets unabashedly championed the war, using whatever language (and symbolism) they felt best served that cause – and never expressed regret. Fox News inserted an American flag in the upper left corner of its screen and referred to the Iraq War by the moniker chosen at the Pentagon: "Operation Iraqi Freedom." CBS News anchorman Dan Rather joined the march, telling Larry King on a TV show broadcast on April 4, 2003: "Look, I'm an American. . . . When my country is at war, I want my country to win. . . . I can't and don't argue that that is coverage without prejudice. About that I am prejudiced."

It is critical that the words used to identify those attacking the U.S. military and those being attacked by U.S. forces be precise. Careless use of prejudicial language can heedlessly skew interpretations of news and history, such as the experiences of the soldiers whose stories I recount here.

In late 2003 the *Los Angeles Times* ordered its reporters to cease using "resistance fighters" when reporting on Iraqi attacks on U.S. forces. Assistant managing editor Melissa McCoy sent her staff an e-mail saying that because "the phrase evoked a certain feeling . . . a certain romanticism or heroism," she didn't want it used to describe the Iraqis resisting U.S. troops. And McCoy issued a credible warning about the possibility of unintentional consequences: "Sometimes certain combinations of words send an unintended signal. You combine these two seemingly innocuous words and suddenly they have this unintended meaning." [10]

She assigned her staff to use instead the words "insurgent" and "guerrilla."

At the *Washington Post*, foreign editor David Hoffman disagreed. "They are resisting an American occupation, so it's accurate," he said about "resistance fighters." He pointed out the myriad of types striking out at Americans. "We try to be as precise as possible and distinguish whether they are former Baath party, Fedayeen, outsiders, insiders. But that's not always possible." [11]

Perhaps the most neutral words to describe people engaged in armed conflict are "fighters" and "militants" and "combatants," apolitical words that do not connote good guys or bad guys. But "enemy" is the word I've decided to use for the opposing forces in Iraq. "Enemy" is the correct word because, although it may not feel so, the word is neutral, and it includes all of those engaged in conflict in Iraq, armed and unarmed.

The origin of the word "enemy" is the Latin *inimicus*, literally "not friend." In modern American English, "enemy" is the best word I've found for those who attack U.S. soldiers. It means someone who intends injury to another. Some Iraqi fighters are common criminals, others believe themselves to be dedicated freedom fighters, and still others are crazed jihadists. But they all are the enemy of U.S. armed forces operating in Iraq, and U.S. soldiers are their enemy.

Perhaps Pogo said it best: "We have met the enemy and he is us."

Immediately following the September 11 attacks, the unity and support of the world community was best expressed by the headline in *Le Monde*, the Paris newspaper usually critical of U.S. foreign policy: "We are all Americans." No longer. The Bush administration's war policies not only destroyed that international solidarity, but, as the true stories of unnecessary pain and anguish in this book make tragically clear, those policies also damaged and destroyed too many of America's and Iraq's most valuable asset: the next generation.

And for what?

Peter Laufer
Sonoma County, California
February 2006

JOSHUA KEY

"I Broke the Rules by Having a Conscience"

"We was going along the Euphrates River," says Joshua Key, a twenty-seven-year-old former U.S. soldier from Oklahoma, detailing a recurring nightmare – a scene he stumbled on shortly after the U.S. invasion of Iraq in March 2003. "It's a road right in the city of Ramadi. We turned a real sharp right and all I seen was decapitated bodies. The heads laying over here and the bodies over here and U.S. troops in between them. I'm thinking, 'Oh my God, what in the hell happened here? What's caused this? Why in the hell did this happen?' We get out and somebody was screaming, 'We fucking lost it here!' I'm thinking, 'Oh, yes, somebody definitely lost it here.'"

Joshua says he was ordered to look around for evidence of a firefight, for something to rationalize the beheaded Iraqis. "I look around just for a few seconds and I don't see anything." But then he noticed the sight that now triggers his nightmares. "I see two soldiers kicking the heads around like a soccer ball. I just shut my mouth, walked back, got inside the tank, shut the door, and it was like, I can't be no part of this. This is crazy. I came here to fight and be prepared for war but this is outrageous. Why did it happen? That's just my question: Why did that happen?"

He's convinced there was no firefight that led to

the beheading orgy – there were no spent shells to indicate a battle. "A lot of my friends stayed on the ground, looking to see if there was any shells. There was never no shells, except for what we shot. I'm thinking, Okay, so they just did that because they wanted to do it. They got trigger happy and they did it. That's what made me mad in Iraq. You can take human lives at a fast rate and all you have to say is, say, 'Oh, I thought they threw a grenade. I thought I seen this, I thought I seen that.' You could mow down twenty people each time and nobody's going to ask you, 'Are you sure?' They're going to give you a high five and tell you that you was doing a good job."

He still cannot get the scene out of his head. "You just see heads everywhere," he says. "You wake up, you'll just be sitting there, like you're in a foxhole. I can still see Iraq just as clearly as it was the day I was there. You'll just be on the side of a little river running through the city, trash piled up, filled with dead. Heads and stuff like that. I don't sleep that much, you might say. I don't sleep that much." His wife, Brandi, nods in agreement and says he cries in his sleep.

We're sitting in the waning summer light on the back porch of the Toronto house where Joshua and his wife and their four little children have been living in exile since Joshua deserted to Canada. They've settled in a rent-free basement apartment, courtesy of a landlord sympathetic to their plight. Joshua smokes cigarettes and drinks coffee while we talk. He's wearing a T-shirt promoting a 2002 peace rally in Raleigh, North Carolina. There's a scraggly beard on his still-boyish face; his eyes look weary.

Sleep deprivation while on duty, first in Kuwait and then in Iraq, was routine, Joshua says, and he thinks exhaustion was generated intentionally by his commanders. "You'll do whatever the hell they say just to get that sleep. That's the way they controlled us. You ain't had no sleep and you got shitty food all the time. I got to call my wife once every month, maybe once every two weeks if I was lucky. Mail, shitty, if it even came." Food and water were inadequate, he says. "When we first got to Kuwait we were rationed to two bottles of water a day and one MRE [meals ready to eat]. In the middle of the desert, you're supposed to have six bottles of water a day and three MREs. They tell us they don't have it. I'm thinking 'How in the hell can the most powerfullest nation, the most powerfullest military in the world, be in the middle of a damn desert and they don't even have no food to feed us?'"

Joshua rejects the U.S. government line that the Iraqis fighting the occupation are terrorists. "I'm thinking: What the hell? I mean, that's not a terrorist. That's the man's home we killed. That's his son, that's the father, that's the mother, that's the sister. Houses are destroyed. Husbands are detained and wives don't even know where they're at. I mean, them are pissed-off people, and they have a reason to be pissed off. I would never wish this upon myself or my family, so why would I do it upon them?"

Pulling security duty in the Iraqi streets, Joshua found himself talking to the locals. He was surprised by how many spoke English, and he was frustrated by the military regulations that forbade his accepting dinner invitations to join Iraqis for social evenings in their homes. "I'm not your perfect killing machine," he admits. "That's where I broke the rules. I broke the rules by having a conscience." And the conscience developed further the more time he spent in Iraq. "I was trained to be a total killer. I was trained in booby-traps, explosives, landmines, and how to counterresolve everything." He pauses. "Hell, if you want to get technical about it, I was made to be an American terrorist. I was trained in everything a terrorist is trained to do." In case I might have missed his point, he says it again. "I mean terrorist."

Deserting to Canada seemed the only viable alternative, Joshua says. He did it, he insists, because he was lied to "by my president." Iraq – it was obvious to him – was no threat to the United States. He says he followed his orders while he was in Iraq, and so no one can call him a coward for deserting. "I was not a piece of shit. I always did everything I was told and I did it to the highest standards. They can never say, 'Oh, he was a piece of shit soldier.' No bullshit."

Joshua doesn't mind telling his war stories again and again. He readily agrees to talk about the horrors he experienced in Iraq, his life AWOL and underground in the States, and his new life as a deserter in Canada. Telling the stories helps him deal with his post-traumatic stress disorder (PTSD), he says, and he apologizes in advance if his narrative is not linear or if he has trouble expressing himself. In fact, his scattered approach to his timeline and his machine gun–like delivery set the scene for his troubled memories – there is nothing smooth or simple or easy to understand here.

He cannot pinpoint when he decided that the war was wrong and that he could no longer serve as a soldier. Joshua served for eight months in Iraq, beginning in April 2003. He was on duty west of Baghdad in Ramadi, Fallujah, Al-Kahim, along Highway 10, working as a combat engineer. "Explosives and land mines, that was my job," he says. This was before the worst days in Fallujah, before it became the scene of fierce opposition to the occupation and of a devastating American military reaction. "Fallujah was very unstable at the time, a lot of sporadic gunfire and a lot of firefights and stuff like that. The way I look at it, we sort of caused what happened there. You know, I think as in most areas we did."

How?

"Innocent people started dying for no reason. Mass casualties. What else is going to happen except total chaos? I seen it with my own eyes. The whole month of May [2003] it was very calm, hardly ever any gunfire. I never got in a firefight the first month I was there; I didn't even know what it was. At the end of May," he says, and then pauses. "When I first got to Iraq, I was in Ramadi." Another pause. "I'm sorry, I jump a lot around."

He tries again. "We went to Ramadi first – that's where I learned how to raid homes, do traffic control points," he says. "That's where they sort of got us into the groove of what we're going to do here. That's where I did my first raid. When we got to Fallujah, that was a total different story."

His unit was trigger-happy, Joshua recalls, and that led to another horrific incident that haunts him to this day. Joshua was in an armored personnel carrier when an Iraqi man in a truck cut them off by making a wrong turn. His squad leader started firing at the truck. "The first shot, the truck sort of started slowing down," Joshua recounts. "And then he shot the next shot, and when he shot that next shot it, you know, exploded."

Joshua watched the truck turn to debris. "It was very strange. He was just going along and just because he tried to cut in front of us. . . . No kind of combat reasons or anything of such. . . . I think he had plenty of distance and everything. . . ." Joshua seems still in shock at the utter senselessness of it all. "Why did it happen and what was the cause for it?" He says it again, "Why? When I asked that question I was told, basically, 'You just didn't see anything, you know?' Nobody asked no questions."

It was symptomatic of what he would see repeatedly in Iraq. "You don't have to have a reason to do anything," he says. "You can do whatever you want, really. I mean, all you have to have is, I guess, the rank to pull it off."

Before he set foot in Iraq, Joshua supported the removal of Saddam Hussein. "They made it sound like one day he's going to be stepping on our doorsteps back home," he says. "I figured, just do it now rather than my kids have to deal with it later on in life. But once we got there, you start seeing it's not what it was kicked up to be. It wasn't like they portrayed it."

Assigned to raid houses, Joshua was quickly conflicted by the job. "It got very traumatic for me, because at first it's like an adrenaline rush. You're thinking, 'Okay, I can do this. I ain't never been trained for it, but of course this is what I got to do, so we'll do it.'"

Most raids started with a briefing. "They would take you into the CO's [commanding officer's] tent. They'd sit you down, you'd have aerial photographs of the place, satellite photos. You'd have a lot of intelligence telling you, you know, what's supposedly going to be there, what they think might be there."

Once at the home to be raided, Joshua started the operation. "Since, myself, I knew demolition, usually we'd put C4 [plastic explosive] on the door, blow the door off and we'd go in – in six-man teams, usually. We would go in, completely raid the home, get all pertinent people out of the home, you know women, children, men. If they look over the age of sixteen you take them and put them in back of a five-ton [truck]. There would be another squad out there that would tie them up, put them in the back, and they'd be sent off. But we couldn't really tell their ages. Sometimes you would have an interpreter with you, but you could never tell if he was telling you the truth or not."

I ask him to describe a typical scene after he blows

the front door and his comrades rush into the house.

"Oh, very traumatic," he says without hesitation. "Yes, very, very traumatic. I mean, yeah, they're screaming and hollering out their lungs."

"And you can't understand a word they're saying?" I ask.

"No, you can't."

"And you're yelling back at them in English?"

"Exactly."

"And they can't understand a word you're saying?"

"No. And it's traumatic on both parts because you got somebody yelling at you, which it might be a woman. You're yelling back at her, telling her to get on the ground or get out of the house. She don't know what you're saying and vice versa. Yeah, you don't know anything. It got to me. We're the ones sending their husbands or their children off, and when you do that it gets even more traumatic because then they're distraught. You know – very, very distraught. Of course, you can't comfort them because you don't know what to say. And that bothered me."

While the residents are restrained, the search progresses. "Oh, you completely destroy the home – completely destroy it," he says. "If there's like cabinets or something that's locked, you kick them in. The soldiers take what they want, at will you might say. You completely ransack it. After you do it, usually a whole other team comes in and does the whole same thing again, just to make sure it's not got anything."

Joshua estimates he participated in about one hundred raids – every one of them a bust.

"I never found anything in a home. You might find one AK-47, but that's for personal use. But I never once found the big caches of weapons they supposed were there. I never once found members of the Baath party, terrorists, insurgents. We never found any of that.

"We would get where they would do whole neighborhoods like that; for no suspicion whatsoever, they would corridor off the whole big neighborhood and do a hundred houses at once." He looks pained at the memories.

The house raids became routine work for him – and they bothered him long after they were done. "Yeah, that was one of my problems when I came home," he says. "That's what I deal with now, because now when I think back, I especially see them people's faces when you raid their home. It got to where it was distraughting to me because I didn't want to do it, but yet I was made to do it. You want to have sympathy towards the people because you know there's no reason in doing this, but you can't, you can't even show it."

But it wasn't only Iraqis who were victims, as Joshua witnessed. "I had three good friends get their legs blown off." It happened during a firefight Joshua missed because he had been up the entire night before, pulling guard duty. When the squad returned, he saw that "one of them's leg was gone from the waist down, two from the knee down. It was crazy. It was a very crazy situation. I always remember when they set it [the leg] right there by him. He just said, 'Well, I get to see my daughter now.' And I'm thinking, 'Oh, shit.

Your leg's blown off.' But his daughter was born while we was there; he never got to see her and that's the way he felt."

It was a sentiment Joshua tells me he understood completely. "I don't know how many times we was in a firefight and I tried to throw myself in front of a shot, just trying to get wounded, just to go home. I think a lot of us do that."

I try to lighten up the moment, just to give us a breather from his ghastly stories. "You're a bad shot in reverse? You can't get yourself shot?"

"Exactly," he tells me. "It'd be funny because I'd see my friends doing it as well. You know, you get in a firefight and you just sort of hope enough of it grabs you that you're not one to get seriously hurt, but you want to get the hell out of there."

Eight months in Iraq and Joshua Key was never hit. In addition to the house raids, he worked a lot of TCPs – traffic control points – checking cars for weapons and other contraband, and he never took a hit. But some of the Iraqis driving up to the TCPs did.

"We had an incident where a vehicle was coming," he tells me. "At that time we didn't have signs, we didn't have anything stating 'Stop,' no interpreters. We had nothing. The only things we had was waving our hands and telling them to stop. One car came through and they totally let loose on the car. After they had hit it, our medic was trying to bandage them up as quick as possible – it was a kid and his father. The father, I'm sure he was dead. The kid looked like he was still breathing. We bandaged them up, put them in the back of our tank, and hauled them to the hospital. At the same time, the other people was checking the vehicle to see if there was weapons or a reason why they didn't stop, and there was nothing. That hit us all hard, because it's just a language barrier. They don't know what the hell we're saying. I'm not going to sit here and kill all of them, you know? And I didn't. A lot of times I wouldn't. They just don't understand. You can't kill everybody. And that's the problem now, you know."

Joshua lets loose with a stream-of-consciousness barrage of war memories and policy critiques, ending with, "You know, stuff like that. With our friends getting their legs blown off. I'm not seeing no gain from all this. I'm fighting a war for months and months. All I'm seeing is death, destruction, and chaos."

A soldier's life was never Joshua Key's dream. He was living in Guthrie, Oklahoma, just looking for a decent job, and he found the Army.

"We had two kids at the time and my third boy was on the way," he says matter-of-factly. "There's no work there. You know what I mean? There wasn't going to be a future. Of course you can get a job working at McDonald's, but that wasn't going to pay the bills." The local Army recruiting station beckoned and Joshua says, "I started thinking, hey, you always see it on TV. I'll go up and I'll talk to them and see what they have to offer."

Joshua looks back on his initial meeting at the recruiting station with regret, remembering himself as an idealistic young man who brushed aside warnings from his friends and family about the Army and decided to choose Uncle Sam over Ronald McDonald. "I know I did the wrong thing because I felt that the man in the green suit – the person with the government – was going to be telling me the truth. I mean, that's what the hell you think. You always hear, 'Don't ever listen to the recruiters. You know they lie to you and shit.' But I'm thinking, 'This guy works for the government. I'm going to listen to what he's got to say.' And he said, 'You have to join right now because if they know that you got a third child on the way, they won't let you in. So you got to do it real quick.' So I was like, 'Let's jump on the ball!'"

Joshua signed up, and says the Army offered him a "nondeployable duty station" and training as a combat engineer – which they defined as a bridge builder – if he relinquished his claim on a signing bonus. He jumped on another ball and picked Fort Carson, Colorado.

He was in for a few surprises when he got to basic training and met the drill sergeants. "I realized that this is a bunch of shit," he says. "They're like, 'Hey, you're going be the baddest killer on the battlefield.' And I'm thinking, 'Oh shit.' I wrote my wife – we still have the letter in storage back in the States – and said, 'Oh shit, I fucked up here, because I thought I was going to be building bridges.' I learned real quick that you don't have the authority to question shit. I mean the only thing you have the authority to question is, 'When can I go to the bathroom?' When I got to Fort Carson, they put me in a rapid deployment unit. I'm thinking, 'What the hell? I thought this was a nondeployable base.' I said to my lieutenant, 'Sir, I've been lied to ever since I got in the Army.' That's when I was told, 'Shut the hell up. You're going to learn the Army way.'"

A high school graduate, Joshua certainly was aware when he joined that the Army is in the war business, a fact he readily admits. "Of course I knew I might have to go to war. I accepted that fact even though they said I wouldn't." But he was unaware of the growing hostilities between the Bush administration and Iraq. "I hardly ever looked at a newspaper. Never watched the news."

And shortly after he finished basic training, he was en route to the war zone. After eight months of fighting he received two weeks off, relief time back in the United States. At the end of that leave, he was due for another Iraq tour.

He never reported for duty.

I ask him how he made that decision. "On the whole way home, from the time I left Baghdad, I never slept one inch," he says. "I'm just thinking, trying to contemplate, because I knew this was my one chance. At that point I knew, this is morally wrong. I can't keep doing this. I'm not going to kill innocent people just because I have to follow my damn orders. I wasn't going to do it."

He follows this memory of his trip home with a rather astounding revelation. "For the last three months I was there, my gun didn't work and I never said a word," he tells me. "I was in constant different battles here and there, and my gun didn't even work. I said something one time. I said, 'You know, my weapon's not working.' They never said anything back. For the last three months I was there I had a faulty weapon, wouldn't even shoot."

He would have shot at an enemy, he tells me, to keep "my ass alive" and "to help my buddies." He would have grabbed another gun. "But otherwise I'm not going to try and kill people. The objective is staying alive." Joshua sometimes speaks in present tense, as if he is still in Iraq. Other times he speaks in past tense and the war he left behind sounds like long ago history. "It's not you're wanting to kill people, it's just you're having to because you're forced to, but yet you're not wanting to. I mean, you're doing what you have to to stay alive."

Joshua still does not understand what he was doing in Iraq in the first place. "I still couldn't tell you why I was there. What purpose was it for? Whose gain was it for? I don't know the truth to it. Like I tell my wife, that's the problem with war – your president, your generals, they send you off to go fight these battles. And all the way down to your commanding officers, they don't go out there with you. They send you out there to fight and do the crazy shit and do the dirty stuff. You're the one who has to live with the nightmares from it. You come back, you're nothing, you know? Guys are living on the streets that fought in Iraq just as well as I did. I mean it's horrific."

A few days after returning to his base in Colorado, Joshua told Brandi that he was convinced the war was wrong, immoral. He made an anonymous call to Fort Carson officials and asked about the possibility of not getting sent back to Iraq, about reassignment to a job stateside. He was told to get back on the plane to Baghdad. Instead he said to Brandi, "The only option we got is running."

The two of them packed up their three children and ran, with the intention of getting far from familiar Colorado. For six hundred dollars they bought a 1978 Camaro and headed east. Joshua wanted to go home to Oklahoma but figured the military would look for him at his mother's house first. The family ran out of money in Philadelphia and Joshua found work as a welder. They lived an underground lifestyle for over a year, frequently checking out of one hotel and into another, worried that if they stayed too long at one place they would attract the kind of attention that would lead to capture.

"I was paranoid," Joshua says. He was perpetually afraid of getting caught, and he was second-guessing his decision to go AWOL. "Every day I asked myself the question, 'Should I go to jail?'" And every day he had the answer for himself: "Why the hell should I have to go to jail, spend any time in prison, for something I totally believe in? It's immoral to me." He continues to share his internal monologue. "And hell, I went there and served my damn time. I had to do things for the wealth of other people. I mean, just leave me the hell alone. That's how I felt about it, but I knew it wasn't going to happen like that. I knew that it might not be now, it might be five years from now, but they're going to come knocking on that door. Wherever the hell we're at, they're going to come knocking. That's when I started checking into things in Canada."

The research was easy. Joshua sat down at a computer, went online, and searched for "deserter needs help to go AWOL." Up popped details about Army Specialist Jeremy Hinzman's flight north and his case for refugee status (along with several websites about George W. Bush's service in the National Guard during the Vietnam War and whether he went AWOL or fulfilled his commitment).

Joshua and Brandi talked it through and decided to opt for a new life as Canadians. It was a difficult choice.

"I know that I'm not going to be able to go back there," he tells me in his Toronto backyard. "I hated leaving my country." He misses his family and he blames the Bush administration. "I blame them because they made me do it," he says flatly. "You can lie to the world; you can't lie to a person who's seen it. They made me have to do things that a man should never have to do, for the purpose of their gain. Not the people's – *their* financial gain."

George W. Bush should be the one to go to prison, says Joshua. "On the day he goes to prison, I'll go sit in prison with him," he says. "Let's go. I'll face it for that music. But that ain't never going to happen." He laughs.

While waiting for the Canadian government to adjudicate his refugee request, Joshua took his wife and children on a road trip from Toronto to Vancouver. It was half vacation and half speaking tour to drum up support for granting U.S. deserters refugee status in Canada. The family stopped off in Winnipeg, where Joshua was the guest on a radio talk show, telling his story and responding to callers' questions – many of whom were hostile.[12]

"Did you not take an oath at the beginning of your service to serve your country?" asked a caller named Dave.

"Yes, I did," answered Joshua. "And I signed up voluntarily. But I never once in that oath said I would invade another country or fight a war for the greed of my president."

Geoff Currier, the show host, jumped into the fray. When you join, he pointed out, you agree to do whatever the Army tells you to do.

"A soldier should have a right to a conscience as well," Joshua shot back. "You shouldn't have to do everything you're told to do. If it's killing civilian people, because you're a soldier you should be implicated in that? No, I don't think so."

Plenty of the callers welcomed Joshua to Canada, but plenty didn't.

"When you enter the military, you're not allowed to have an opinion," said a caller named Rick with harsh irritation in his voice. "You're not allowed to voice your concerns, you know that going in. They've fed you, they've clothed you, and they've schooled you. Now you've come to Canada. Well, we don't want you either, buddy, honest to God." Rick said he'd like to throw Joshua out of the country himself.

The next day, says Joshua, the two encountered

each other at a Winnipeg peace demonstration. "I was speaking and he presented himself to me and told me that he was in the Vietnam War. He said he had thought it out and that he was sorry, that he understands my reasoning."

As he adjusts to his new life in Canada, Joshua Key says he continues to suffer through flashbacks and nightmares from his days in Iraq. And while he and Brandi hope for a peaceful future in Canada, they look back with sadness at their native land.

"I think it was terrible we had to leave our country," he says. "But we did what we had to do. I love my people. I love the American people. I love the American land. But I do not like the American government."

2

COMING HOME

Joshua Key is just one of an enormous number of Iraq War veterans suffering post-traumatic stress disorder. Returning home psychologically damaged is as old as war. Gregory Peck sums up war-caused trauma succinctly in a brief speech in the 1956 film, *The Man in the Gray Flannel Suit*. In the scene, Tommy, Peck's character, is picking up his life after fighting in World War II. He suffers combat flashbacks on the commuter train to and from his office job, and at home his wife (played by Jennifer Jones) tells him he has changed since the war.

"I suppose I have, in a way," he says to her. And then he explains why. "I was what we have to have in our country, a citizen soldier. One day a man is catching the 8:26 and suddenly he's killing people. And a few weeks later he's catching the 8:26 again. It'd be a miracle if it didn't change him in some way."

The National Center for Post-Traumatic Stress Disorder defines PTSD as "a psychiatric disorder that can occur following the experience or witnessing of life-threatening events such as military combat, natural disasters, terrorist incidents, serious accidents, abuse (sexual, physical, emotional, ritual), and violent personal assaults like rape. People who suffer from PTSD often relive the experience through nightmares and flashbacks, have difficulty sleeping, and feel detached or estranged, and these symptoms can be severe enough and last long enough to significantly impair the person's daily life."

A 2004 study commissioned by the Army estimated that one out of every six soldiers who fought in the Iraq War came home with PTSD.[13] The Veterans Administration (VA) responded with treatments designed to help these soldiers deal with the psychological damage they suffered in Iraq, and to cope with what researchers found was one of the most serious barriers to treatment: the veterans' fear that seeking help would make them be seen as unreliable, weak, and cowardly, and, worse, would harm their careers. Typical PTSD symptoms for war veterans include severe difficulties readjusting to domestic life, spousal abuse and failed personal relationships, poor on-the-job performance, and alcoholism.

Unlike veterans of previous wars, some Iraq War veterans received treatment for PTSD while the war continued and at a time when they were susceptible to being redeployed to the battlefields. "In some cases it makes them very shy about getting any treatment," Dr. Marion Eakin, a VA psychiatrist and PTSD specialist in New York City, says about soldiers she treats who suffer PSTD symptoms while still in the military. "They get very anxious. They're worried about what's going to go on their record and how it's going to affect their standing." And Dr. Eakin confirms Joshua Key's motivation for enlisting. "A lot of them have joined the military for a career, for an opportunity, to get away from backgrounds that are less than privileged. They're worried about being labeled as having some mental problem." When we talk in late 2005, her caseload of Iraq War victims is increasing exponentially, and the VA is devising schemes to reach out to those PTSD sufferers hesitant about seeking treatment. Although some of the soldiers she works with express a readiness to return to the war zone, others make clear their profound opposition to a war that made them ill and jeopardized their lives.

"One guy I saw last week, for example, told me he used to love being in the service," she says. "This is a guy who was in the Marine Corps, the Army, and then he joined the National Guard because he wanted to be closer to his daughter. Then he got deployed to Iraq. He's in his mid-thirties. He said, 'The one thing I'm really good at is the military and now I don't know what else I can do.' He said, 'I was really proud to serve my country, but now when I look at what is happening in Iraq, I feel like some of the work I did over there is a waste.'" Dr. Eakin says this patient's frustration was not so much with the overall mission or the war itself but with the results. "He felt he had worked really hard and made a lot of sacrifices, and that ground was not being gained."

The combination of stresses and strains in this soldier's life brewed a mess for his return to the civilian world. "This guy has a real problem with domestic violence. He has nightmares. He's a very angry young man. He has a hair-trigger temper. He said, 'I would actually never do it, but I just feel like shooting people some of the time.' He just can't get out of that battle mode." Dr. Eakin sounds resigned as she recounts the soldier's litany of problems; she's heard from a long line of veterans with variations on the same theme. "He was treating his relationship like he was the commander and the spouse was the inferior who has to obey orders." In addition to his Iraq experiences, he had been physically abused as a child. This combination tends to make war veterans more prone to develop PTSD. He suffers nightmares about the war and experiences flashbacks: He's driving down the road and sees debris in the road and thinks it's a roadside bomb.

Treatment for a damaged Iraq War veteran like this one is a challenge for Dr. Eakin and her team. "This is a guy who doesn't believe in medications, who doesn't believe a whole lot in mental health treatment. In this particular situation, because his relationship – which was everything to him – has fallen apart because of domestic violence, he himself is motivated to get some counseling in anger management. He doesn't have interest in long-term treatment, but he realizes now that he needs help."

Anger is a common problem for soldiers suffering from PTSD, and the VA offers behavior modification programs designed to treat out-of-control anger. That anger often is exacerbated by sleep disorders and nightmares and is routinely treated with drugs. Unfortunately, many psychiatric medications can lead to weight gain and depressed sexual functioning, side effects that drive patients away from trying the drugs that can relieve their sufferings.

Dr. Eakin is hearing plenty of complaints about

logistics in the Iraq area of operations from her clients, but not much about politics and policy: "A lot of them say it was disorganized. They don't think the leadership was good. They felt inadequately supported. Most of the ones I'm seeing are entangled in their own stories and their own personal adjustment problems. That's what they talk about. Many are proud of what they did for the most part, but it was hard. One guy said, 'First we were told to shoot anything. They kept changing the rules on us. Then we were told to shoot only at armed people. Then we were told only to shoot if we were shot at first.' He was a Marine and he found these changing instructions very upsetting."

Dr. Eakin describes another PTSD patient as a Boy Scout leader, a super-nice guy, very responsible. "He went over there and he tells these stories about the women and children he saw. In particular, a woman came toward him with the burnt torso of her dead child and said to him, in English, 'Baby! Baby!' as if, he thought, she was asking him to put her baby back together again. He thinks about that every day. He's haunted by the image of this woman, whose child had been hit by a mine. Those images haunt him. About what he did overall," she muses, "he hasn't really talked about that yet." Dr. Eakin doesn't ask. The wounds are too deep and too fresh. "Some of the ones who are really sick – to start questioning what they did in Iraq would be very hard for them at this time, while they're just trying to adjust to being back."

Over time, she says, in therapy, these patients need

help putting their war experiences into the context of their lives. "They don't seem very rah-rah about the war." Nonetheless, "some of them want to go back, they would go back." Because the VA is treating these PTSD sufferers early, and because Americans, even if they oppose the war, generally support the troops as individuals, Dr. Eakin is guardedly optimistic that many of her patients will recover and enjoy a successful return to society, that their reentry will not be as difficult as it was for Vietnam War veterans. The VA and the society at large have learned from mistakes made a generation ago. "I think they can come out and function. I don't think they're untouched. I don't think they'll be totally fine after what they've been through. It changes them." But some will, she's convinced, fall through the cracks – casualties of the war.

"I too have nightmares," says Abdul Henderson, an Iraq War veteran, during his speech to the 2005 Veterans for Peace conference near Dallas. "I've talked to a lot of old Vietnam-era veterans and I asked them, 'Were you angry after you came back?' They're like, 'Man, it's been thirty-five years and I'm still angry!'" The crowd laughs a knowing laugh. "Having to see the things I did and having to do the things I did in the name of defending our country puts a deep pain in my heart."

Abdul grew up in Los Angeles, playing with his GI Joe doll and dreaming of a military career. He watched *Top Gun* and figured being a Navy pilot was a nifty goal but then decided the Marines were more glorious. He enlisted after some college, hoping to fly. His motivation was not money but dreams of glory and service to country. Early in 2003 he was deployed to Kuwait, just in advance of the invasion of Iraq. "I was against the war before the war even started," he says. "We put sanctions on Iraq in '93. They couldn't import any military hardware. We were constantly bombing the country in the no-fly zone. If a man can't control his own air space, I don't think he'd be a serious threat to our own country. It didn't make sense. He was really confined to Baghdad." The insistence by the Bush administration that Saddam Hussein maintained mobile biological weapons labs and other weapons of mass destruction under such conditions was not credible. "But out of duty and obligation to my country, when my president ordered me to active duty I answered that call."

Pleasantly serious, Abdul says he opposes the Iraq War, not the military: "That's one thing a lot of people get mixed up. I'm protesting this war. I'm not really antiwar. Sometimes war is inevitable. I love the Marine Corps. To this day I love the Marine Corps."

But the Marine Corps did not take too well to Abdul being featured in the Michael Moore documentary *Fahrenheit 9/11*. The two of them stationed themselves outside the Capitol building and buttonholed members of Congress, asking them why their own sons and daughters were not fighting in the war they had sanctioned in Iraq. And the lance corporal told Moore on camera that if he were ordered to go back to Iraq, he would refuse: "I would not let anyone send me back over there to kill other poor people, especially when they pose no threat to me or my country." Following that brief appearance in the film, his career in the Marines ended. The Marine Corps decided not to press charges against him for his in-uniform remarks; he was discharged for injuries he received during his two months of duty in Iraq, duty that earned him the Marine Corps Achievement Medal.

For Abdul, a continuing puzzle after he returned from Iraq was the quiet about the war from his generation. "Why aren't young people involved in this? The only thing I can really think of is young people are consumed with worrying about self." Too many are politically apathetic and don't vote, he says, and don't keep track of the news that ultimately affects them: not just the war, but also budget deficits and Social Security and other long-term issues. He sounds like the politician he's become – his eyes are on the California state assembly, for starters – as he gently criticizes young voters for their short-term interest in buying a house and car, traveling, and enhancing their own lives at the expense of society. "Maybe they truly feel that they can't make a difference," he muses. "I think that they're having a hard time trying to figure out what is the truth."

He speculates that one reason is that "the marketing is different" with the Iraq War than it was with Vietnam. "You don't see the end of a bombing strike. And if you do see it, you have to go on the internet to pull it up and download it," he says. "They don't show this on public media like they used to. The public media used to show all these atrocities. You saw the real horror – the innocent kids in Vietnam with bullet wounds and blood. The true effects of what happens at a suicide bombing. The people here," he says about being back home, "don't have to feel that stress. Our media has done a very good job of suppressing our stress."

Charlie Anderson became intrigued by the military watching *GI Joe* cartoons on television while growing up in Toledo, and he still remembers the channel and the times in the afternoon on which the show was broadcast. Looking back on that early influence, he recalls no bullets being shot on the show, and no combatants dying. "We used to watch *GI Joe* [and] we would go play war," he says. By high school he'd read a lot of books about war, including enough about the Vietnam War to believe it wrong, but he still considered the soldiers heroic. He was accepted at Purdue University, but decided not to go and instead stocked shelves at a store, wondering what to do with his life. In 1996, a recruiter gave him a ride to work one day, and without much trouble signed him up.

Assigned to a Marine infantry battalion, Charlie trained as a medic and enjoyed a tour of the Mediterranean during the calm just prior to September 11, 2001. A large-framed man, he's lost some of his fighting trim, and his black hair is thinning. He speaks in rapid bursts, accompanied by jerky body movements, and often refers to his post-traumatic stress disorder, which led to his retirement from the Navy after he served in Iraq.

He is also participating in the Veterans for Peace

conference near Dallas in the summer of 2005, and
Charlie is telling the story of his arrival in Kuwait on
February 2, 2003, just before the invasion of Iraq.
Tents were set up by Indian and Pakistani contract
workers. "Let the *hajjis* do it," Charlie heard for the
first time, something he only later recognized as "the
beginning of the dehumanizing process" of the
people he was sent overseas to fight. (The term is
derived from the *Haj* – the pilgrimage to Mecca that
Muslims must make at least once during their
lifetimes. *Hajji* is a title of honor amongst Muslims,
but it was a derogatory slur when used by some U.S.
forces in Iraq.)

Within weeks, Charlie crossed into Iraq, and the
first casualty he saw was a U.S. soldier killed outside
Nasiriyah by another soldier in his own platoon, an
exhausted buddy who had made an error and shot
the victim three times. That night, says Charlie, he
wrote in his journal, "I don't know if our causes are
just or not. I don't know if the reasons they gave us
are true or not. But this operation has already
become too costly in human life." His first action in
a firefight came in the Sadr City slum of Baghdad. "I
fired my weapon nine times, I shot nine rounds. I
don't know what I shot at. I don't know who or
what was there." He pauses. "And that was really
hard to deal with. I still have trouble dealing with
that today."

As Charlie recounts his time in Iraq, he expresses
himself in random fragments of stories and thoughts.
He tells of his feelings of helplessness when his unit
was attacked. He talks about the soldiers who died –

he feels their sacrifice is unnoticed. He explains how he tried to believe his commanders' insistence that Iraq posed a threat to America. "In October of 2004, they said there's no WMD, and I just sat down and cried. That was the last straw. It was for absolutely nothing," he says about the war. "I felt totally worthless. I sacrificed part of my humanity. People around me sacrificed significantly more than I did. For what? For what? I can't point to a single thing. We're going to liberate the Iraqi people by killing them?"

He was back home by May, but his problems continued. "My daughter had been eight months when I left, she was a year when I got home," he says. "She called me 'Daddy' the night I left. When I saw her the morning after I got home, she cried and ran away from me. She called me 'Mommy' for the next eighteen months. Mommy, Daddy, I don't really care. But there was this loss of a relationship."

"I'm a veteran of Operation Iraqi Plunder," Charlie tells the other veterans when he stands up to make his speech. "I think it is important to tell it like it is. I refuse to call it Operation Iraqi Freedom. There was no freedom over there. It was not a war to liberate Iraq. It was a war to make it safe for U.S. business interests. It was a war of aggression and occupation. To call it Operation Iraqi Freedom is an insult to the Iraqi people and it is an insult to humanity."

And then Charlie tells his story about coming home.

"I thought I was one of the lucky people – I thought I came through the war unscathed," he begins. "When they handed me my plane ticket and said, 'Well done, have a nice day,' I thought that was it. I thought, Thank God I had gotten home, back to my family, and things were going to be okay." He pauses, then adds, "Except I couldn't sleep through the night. I would break down crying for no reason. I would fly off in fits of rage over things that were totally trivial, like who left the bathroom door open." Another pause.

"Something was wrong with me," he says with such dry understatement that it emphasizes the tragedy. "I knew it had to be me because everybody around me was fine. My neighbors were okay. They were in the military. They were over in Iraq. My friends were okay. They were over in Iraq. Then I started talking with some veterans from Vietnam. At first they all kind of broke into these smiles, and I thought, 'Not only am I going crazy, these guys think it's funny.'" A knowing punctuation of laughter comes from the audience as Charlie explains that the Vietnam War veterans told him they understood what was happening to him because it mirrored their experiences. That's when he learned he suffered from PTSD. The military concurred and he was discharged. "People say, 'Oh, you got sick and they threw you out.' And I say, 'No. I was psychologically wounded.'"

The university bells are tolling as Charlie recalls his warm welcome home. "Everyone was thanking us for our service and I was feeling ashamed. I was embarrassed. People were saying, 'I'm proud of what you did over there.' And I'm saying, 'God! I'm not. Why are you telling me you're proud of me? You don't even know what I did.'"

★★★

Back in the early 1980s, a recovering Vietnam War veteran I interviewed offered this lay advice to help the next generation of soldiers coming home with the horrors of war: "Stand out in the streets and throw a ticker tape parade," he urged. "Play a band. Welcome them home. Debrief them. Give them what they need when they get home, don't wait fifteen years until the guy is almost out of his mind with stress that he's been holding in to himself. Give him a chance to vent it when he gets home so he doesn't have to drag it through his life. I think that would have made a big difference for all of us." He repeated his wish quietly before we said good-bye. "I think that would have made a big difference." [14]

3

RYAN JOHNSON
The Unexpected Activist

From the outside, the Catholic Worker house in Toronto's gritty Parkdale neighborhood could charitably be said to be in a state of arrested decay. I'm waiting on the porch for Ryan Johnson, a Californian who has been in Canada with his wife, Jennifer, for just three weeks, having crossed the border after almost six months absent without leave from the Army.

The porch and the stately brick façade of this once-graceful single-family home are in need of paint. A mobile made out of a tree branch hangs from the porch ceiling, with paper disks attached to the pieces of branch that drift in the very slight breeze. On the disks are the words BE and STILL and KNOW and GOD. A bird's nest is on display. The couch and the easy chair on the porch have the look of donated furniture: faded, threadbare, and repaired by amateurs. I can see into the living room, where a wall of shelves is filled with vinyl LPs. Leonard Cohen comes wafting through the window, singing "Suzanne," and "Suzanne" again, and "Suzanne" one more time. The record is skipping.

There is a bohemian feel to Parkdale; it's a Toronto neighborhood in the early stages of gentrification. The house next door on the south side is boarded up. At the end of the block the Gardiner Expressway slices the neighborhood from Lake Ontario and offers a steady rippling murmur of white noise.

Soon, twenty-one-year-old Ryan shows up from the house next door on the north side, another Catholic Worker house. He's wearing a black T-shirt, blue jeans, and black running shoes. He makes himself comfortable in the easy chair, and as we talk his brilliant blue eyes alternate between meeting mine and looking off into the middle distance. He's articulate as we wend through his story.

When Ryan went AWOL in January 2005, he simply went home to Visalia, California. "It was very stressful," he says. "I lived only four hours away from my home base. I figured they could come get me at any time. But they never came by. They never came looking for me. They sent some letters, that's all they did." The military doesn't devote significant manpower to chasing AWOL soldiers and deserters, other than issuing a federal arrest warrant. Those who get caught usually are arrested for something unrelated, their AWOL status revealed when local police enter their names into the National Crime Information Center database – a routine postarrest procedure throughout the United States.

Ryan moved to Canada because he was afraid that if he applied for a job in the United States, a background check would cause him to be arrested, which would mean a criminal record that would make it difficult to find future work. Voluntarily turning himself in to the Army would not have improved his options either. "I had two choices – go to Iraq and have my life messed up, or go to jail and have my life messed up. So I came here to try this out." In fact, he says, it was Jennifer who came up with the plan to cross the border.

Back at his base in the southern California desert, Ryan had listened hard to the stories told by soldiers returning from the war. "I didn't want to be a part of that." His fears and concerns about the war that has been reported to him spill out in a torrent of nightmarish impressions.

"There were people that saw their best friends killed right in front of them. They have to pick them up while they're missing their head and drag them off to a truck," he says. "It traumatizes them for the rest of their lives, you know? They can't work anymore. They have difficulty just talking to other people. But there's also not just watching their friends die, but killing people and watching other people kill people. And it's not people with guns all the time, sometimes it's old women, you know, that are just walking. They think that she might be a threat, so they shoot her and then they find out that she's completely unarmed. Or running over a child that's standing in the middle of the street. I'd heard stories of people that – a vehicle would be coming towards them and it wouldn't be slowing down, so 'Light it up,' you know, they'd blow the truck, the car, up and they'd walk by and find out that there was a young boy driving it and that's all that was in there. I mean, like, horrifying, traumatizing stories. I didn't want to be part of this, because eventually these stories are going to come out, just like in Vietnam, people telling about the bad things that happened over there. I don't want to be lumped in with the people that were committing these things."

I remind him that unlike in the Vietnam era, there was no draft when he became eligible to join the Army. He went down to the Visalia recruiting office and signed up. Did he really not know then that the Army was in the business of killing people?

"That's true, yeah, they are," he acknowledges. "But, like I said, what I didn't understand is how traumatizing it was to actually kill somebody or watch one of your friends get killed. I've never seen anyone die."

"When I joined," he says, and there seems frustration and bitterness in his voice with the memory, "I joined because I was poor." Ryan says jobs were hard to come by in Visalia and he lacked the funds for college. The sign in the strip mall outside the recruiting office beckoned, despite the fact that war already was burning up the Iraqi desert and sending GIs home dead. "I talked to the recruiters. I said, 'What are the chances of me going to Iraq?' They said, 'Depends on what job you get.' Okay, so I said, 'Well what jobs could I get that wouldn't have me go to Iraq?' And they named off jobs. I picked one of those jobs and they said that I probably wouldn't go to Iraq. Plus, they asked me if I had any family members that were deceased. I said my father died, and I'm the only child of my father. They said it's like the *Saving Private Ryan* thing, you don't have to go to Iraq." Ryan keeps rattling off his story, not seeming to notice that he was recruited to *become* Private Ryan by recruiters citing the movie title. "My recruiters told me that I wouldn't have to go because of that," because he is the sole surviving son. "But they didn't tell me that that's only if your father or your brother or sister dies while you're in the service, and they have to die in combat. I didn't know that." Like so many before and after him, Ryan Johnson was too unsophisticated to ask probing questions at the Army recruiting office, and he didn't question many of the answers he did receive, especially those from the woman who signed him up, a smooth-talking Sergeant Quick.

"I didn't have a problem serving my country," says Ryan, "but I didn't want to go and fight. I didn't want to kill people. When I found out I was being shipped to Iraq, I was still going to go because I signed up and all that." But it was the war stories from returning soldiers that convinced him otherwise. "I was talking to people that had seen war crimes and beaten prisoners. I was like, No, this isn't right, the things that are happening over there, when people are breaking laws and not being punished for it – like shooting someone in a mosque in front of cameras. They should go to jail. They're not going to do anything to that guy. But the guy that threw a grenade and killed his commander, he's going to jail, because he committed a crime against the U.S."

Ryan insists dying in combat he could handle. "I'm not worrying about dying. I don't care about me dying. But I wouldn't want to come back and have to live the rest of my life either with no arms or no legs or having post-traumatic stress disorder and having difficulty functioning around people that I would normally have a good time with."

Again I suggest these understandable worries were the risks he took when he signed on the dotted line.

"I was twenty years old," he says defensively. "I thought we were rebuilding in Iraq. I thought we were doing good things. But we're blowing up mosques. We're blowing up museums, peoples' homes, all the culture. I mean, I didn't even realize Iraq was, like, Mesopotamia, you know? There's all this culture and everything in Iraq. I never knew that, you know? I like to think of myself as pretty well educated for someone that didn't even graduate high school, but I've never really known anything about history or other cultures."

Ryan says he was a troublemaker in high school who didn't do his homework and didn't pass his tests, wasn't motivated, and eventually just dropped out. Next came a series of dead-end jobs. He was lured to the military partly by Sergeant Quick, who told him stories of the good life in the regular Army. "She told me how five days out of the week you work a nine-to-five job, you go home, you take off your uniform and you're a civilian," he says. "You can go out. Go to a bar. You can go hang out at a pool hall or just watch TV, whatever you feel like doing. She just made it seem like it was really easy to do." He reflects on his own ignorance and innocence. "I found out, obviously, when I got there that it wasn't. You go in at four o'clock in the morning and get off at nine o'clock at night. You do that for six days, you get one day of rest, which most people would want to spend time with their family, but you're too tired."

Once Ryan went AWOL, surrendering to the authorities was not an option in his mind. "I would have had to go to prison. When I got out, I'd have to go live at my mom's house until I got a job. Then when I got a job, I'd probably still live at my mom's house for a long time. And already there are seven people staying at my mom's house. She has a three-bedroom house with seven people in it. And with me and Jennifer there, that'd be nine of us living at my mom's house. I did that for a while and it's just too hard. It's crazy. It puts a strain on everybody and everyone's always fighting. I couldn't do it anymore."

Ryan Johnson hopes to be granted refugee status by the Canadians. If that is denied, he says he'll seek authority to stay for humanitarian reasons. He's waiting for a work permit, which the Canadian authorities are likely to grant him while his refugee claim works its way through the system. Until then, the War Resisters Support Campaign – an ad hoc group of antiwar activists who organized quickly when the trickle of American soldiers avoiding Iraq started north – is providing Ryan and Jennifer with pocket money, and the Catholic Worker organization is housing and feeding them.

Since going AWOL, Ryan has been politicized, and he's now surrounded by a supportive new community in Toronto: other deserters and Canadian volunteers who are helping them resettle. He's prepared with ready answers when he is faced with critics who call his run north an act of cowardice, unpatriotic and a crime.

"The soldiers that are going to Iraq, most of them aren't patriotic," he says. "They aren't going to Iraq because our flag has red, white, and blue on it. They're not going because we think that Iraq is posing a threat to us. Most of us are going because we're ordered to and our buddies are going. That's one of the reasons that I was going to go, because my buddies are over there." And he's immediately wistful when asked how he feels about being safe in peaceful Toronto while those buddies are fighting and dying in the desert: "I check the casualties list every day. Every day I go on the internet and I check the casualties list to see if my friends are on there. And as of yet," he pauses, "seven people from my unit have died, and I knew four of them."

He says he made some close friends during basic training and considers what help he might have been to them were he in Iraq. "Or I wish they were here with me. It really tears me up. I'm scared for them. They were like my family for twenty-six weeks. I slept in the same room with these guys forever. Knowing that they're over there, it's hard. I wish that they weren't in the position to have to be over there." He knows at least one buddy who was actively seeking an alternative to Iraq duty. "He asked me if I'd break his legs so that he didn't have to go to Iraq, because his mother's dying of cancer, and he's over there."

Ryan refused the request and suggested his traumatized friend do what he did: call the GI Rights

Hotline. The Hotline connected Ryan with the San Diego Military Counseling Project. It was three in the morning when he dialed them. The counselor who answered the phone told him the likely consequences of going AWOL, and based on that information off he went. The counselor recommended he not flee to Canada, but visions of poverty and Iraq and jail time eventually motivated him to cross the border.

Back home in Visalia, Ryan's flight to Canada did not go over well. "Everyone cried and they were mad, but the next day they called me back and they were just asking me about Canada, and I've been talking to them ever since. They're supportive of me." Ryan tells me his mother and his little stepbrother and sister want to come up and visit him in Canada, but maybe not for a year. An annual family trip to Disneyland had already been planned for the family vacation time.

We talk more about his family back home, and he lets on that he's not as convinced that their response is as sanguine and supportive as he'd like it be. "My mom, I'm not really sure. . . ." He hesitates. "She's kind of a hard one to figure out. But she seems like she's okay with it except for the fact that it's going to be a while before I can come back to the States."

It's 98 degrees Fahrenheit and the air is still and dry when, a few weeks later, I visit the Visalia that Ryan Johnson ran away from, deep in the agricultural heart of California's San Joaquin Valley. The sleepy farm town is a world away from cosmopolitan Toronto.

I am here to meet Ryan's mother, Crystal Lewis, in a café at a strip mall north of downtown. She shows up wearing blue jeans and a sleeveless shirt festooned with the Disney image of Sleeping Beauty. Sparkling rhinestones dot her eyeglasses.

I tell her Ryan and Jennifer seemed happy together when I saw them in Toronto.

"Yeah, *they're* happy."

"You're not happy about his decision?"

"Not really."

I ask why.

"There was other alternatives."

"What should he have done?" I ask.

"Heck, he could have just gotten fat and gotten kicked out."

It's noisy in the café and I'm not sure I heard her right. "Gotten fat and kicked out?"

"You know," she says, surprised I'm asking for clarification. "I mean, they're kicking them out left and right now because these other guys are smarter than my son, I assume. They're just blowing up like balloons and getting themselves kicked out."

I'm still not sure if she really means overweight or if I'm missing some sort of code or jargon. "You mean that literally? By getting obese?"

"Yeah." [15] She shakes her long red hair back. After Ryan signed up, Crystal tried to convince him to change his mind. "They have so many days when they can back out."

She orders a large mocha latte with whipped cream. "We tried to talk him out of it. Tried to talk him out of it. . . ." Her voice trails off.

"Why did you want to talk him out of it?" I ask.

She looks at me as if I am completely out of touch with reality. "You never join the Army in times of war," she says. Then adds: "Unless you have a death wish."

"So what was his reasoning to you when you tried to talk him out of it?"

"His reasoning for joining was because he could not support her and himself." She makes her opinion clear with her tone – Jennifer is not her favorite. "You know, this isn't the best area, unless you have a damn good education and you're damn lucky. You know, most of the people here that go to college, they move off and get a good paying job because the few good jobs here, people don't want to let loose of them. My husband has worked for UPS for eighteen years."

"That's what Ryan said to me, that he felt it really was a dead end here in terms of his future," I tell her.

Her response is that of a frustrated mother, if somewhat contradictory. "It's not a dead end," she retorts. "You just have to go to school, apply yourself. He joined the Army so he could get an education and they would have a guaranteed income, guaranteed medical. Which is all good and fine, but you don't do it during a time of war."

When Crystal argued against the Army, she says Ryan told her the Army would give him money for school. "I'm, like, going, 'But you may not live to see the education.'" He told her that his job would be working in supply, so even if he were sent to Iraq he wouldn't be on the front lines. "This is a war with no front lines," Crystal knows, "and unfortunately he found that out too late. These two, they think they know everything, and you try and you try and you try and you try to talk to them, but they get something in their mind and they're right."

She recounts to me the drama that entered her life when Ryan first went AWOL. "I wake up at three or four o'clock in the morning to a phone call: 'Mom, I'm on my way.' I'm, like, okay. I was asleep, I didn't know what he meant. Then I get a phone call from his staff sergeant: 'You know your son's AWOL?' And I'm, like, 'Wow, really?'" The staff sergeant asked her if she thought Ryan was en route to Visalia. She told him that she did not know his destination. "At the time I wasn't lying. I didn't even remember the phone call. And then a little while later I'm going, 'Oh my God, no.' It took me probably a good hour after I got a phone call from the staff sergeant for it to occur to me that Ryan called me at some point in the middle of the night saying he was on his way to my house." She wasn't sure she wanted him in her house. "I don't need the military busting my door down."

Ryan and Jennifer showed up in Visalia a few hours later, from Fort Irwin near Barstow. At first they stayed with friends. But those arrangements didn't last long. "He'd come and visit and then go stay with his friends. But since all of his friends are worthless, and they're all living with their parents, he ended up living with us. I guess you could say they were investigating options."

Jennifer and Ryan left Visalia for San Diego and meetings with counselors at the San Diego Military

Counseling Project. Crystal thought Ryan would get a lawyer and seek a discharge based on his history of mental and physical problems. "He had hurt his back, he had hurt his hand. Before he joined he had told them he had had asthma as a child and that he had depression, he had mental problems. And the recruiting sergeant just told him that's been so many years it doesn't matter. I thought he was going to take the legal way out. I don't hear from him for weeks, and then I find out he's in Canada."

Choosing exile was a mistake, Crystal tells me.

"Because first place, he can't come back," she says. "He thinks he can come back in four years after the war ends. But I'm like, 'You've lost your mind. It took twenty-five years for them to allow anybody to come back from the Vietnam War.' I said, 'I could be dead and gone in twenty-five years.' His grandfather won't be here that much longer, neither one of his grandfathers. You know something could happen to his sister or brother. He wouldn't be able to even come and visit. Something could happen to him. Yeah, I could go visiting, but I couldn't bring him home to take care of him."

I tell Crystal that Ryan spoke to me eloquently about his opposition to the war. She is not impressed. "He thinks that he finally got a conscience. That's not what it is." She insists Ryan's flight to Canada was fueled by Jennifer. "I love my son, and he's basically a good person. But these two, they do things and they get themselves into a position that they can't get out of."

Crystal continues to protest Ryan's choice with a

series of complaints – mostly about the way he left and the things he left behind at Fort Irwin. She's been negotiating with his sergeant to retrieve those that are precious to her. "Their furniture and stuff wouldn't have been any big deal, but there was things left back there that really upset me," she says, including family pictures of her and Ryan and his father, quilts that Ryan's great-grandmother had made, even "his grandpa's little can opener from when he was in Korea."

From her frustrated point of view, Ryan should come back to the United States, turn himself in, and go to jail. I'm surprised. "He needs to go to jail?"

"Yeah. Go to jail. I think he needs to turn himself in, go to jail, and just pay his dues," she says emphatically. "I feel if you screw up, pay your dues. Get it over with. Start with a clean slate. That's the way I was brought up. If you steal something, pay for it, you know? And he signed up. He didn't listen to us. He went AWOL. He didn't take anything into consideration. They just walked off. And you can't do that. I mean, you can't go through life like that, running away from everything you create." It is a passionate and heartfelt speech, difficult for a mother to make about her son.

I remind her that Ryan maintains that he came to oppose the Iraq War only after he joined the Army, and that he only learned that the recruiter had lied to him once he was in the service. Crystal is unmoved. "The recruiters didn't exactly lie to him," she says. "They just made it sound like he wouldn't have to go to war. I was there. They told him that he possibly could, but if he did, it would be in a safe zone." She says it again: "They did tell him there was a possibility he could go – I was there.

"I told Ryan that you can't believe anything they tell you because they're going to tell you whatever they have to, to fill those boots," she says with exasperation. "They have boots to fill. He made his bed. He's going to have to learn to grow up. I'm not getting him a lawyer. I don't have the money to pay for a lawyer. You're talking fifty, sixty thousand dollars. I'm not selling my house. I'm not going to harass him and tell him to come back, because he's not going to listen to us anyway."

She is not even sure she's going to make the trip north to visit Ryan, "because I don't like Canadians."

"Why don't you like Canadians?" I ask.

"Because I don't like the anti-American attitude," she explains without hesitation. Not that she supports the war. "I started out thinking we should be there. Now I don't. Only because I don't think our boys should be dying for a bunch of ungrateful sand jockeys. And I can say that, my husband is half Armenian. That's what they call themselves." She laughs, and then takes on the Iraqis again. "They're ungrateful. I don't think we should be there protecting them or doing anything for them any longer. I think we should just get out and protect our own shores and the hell with them. You know what happened this morning in England." We're talking on the summer day in 2005 that the Underground was bombed in London. "You know these people want to get rid of us. It's another Hitler situation. They want to exterminate the white race. We've got to preserve ourselves here."

Her moral quandaries are confounding. But her geopolitical analysis continues with an assault on the French for refusing to join the U.S. attack on Iraq. Let's just "protect our own shores," she tells me, "and let the rest of them go to hell in a hand basket, you know? We saved Europe and we're the bad guys. We're always the bad guys no matter what we do."

As for her son's antiwar philosophy, she dismisses it as an opportunistic act with a sarcastic, "Oh, so he tells you. I hate to be the one" – her voice trails off for a second – "but I'm not going to lie, I'm not going to lie. I was raised up to do what's right. If I bind myself to something, I do it and I don't make an excuse. I mean, honest to God, I don't feel that they're being honest with Canada about why they're there."

Isn't it possible, I suggest to her, that since Ryan went AWOL, since he met with the GI Rights Hotline group in San Diego, since he's been talking with other deserters in Canada, that he has become politicized, that he has – in fact – changed.

"Anything's possible." But she thinks otherwise, and believes he just wants out of the service. "You don't want the Army, you don't want to fight? Fine. But do it the right way. Get yourself fat and get kicked out."

The mocha cup is empty; we've been talking for an hour, and it seems as if she's been further developing her own positions vis-à-vis Ryan and the Iraq War during our conversation. As we say good-bye, her conclusions come out in fragments.

She's against the Iraq War, but not war: "I mean, I

have to admit I'm struggling with things on the war, only because I don't like seeing our boys die. I'm against it. Not because I don't believe in war – I just don't believe we should be over there dying for those people." She blames Ryan for making poor choices, but faults the recruiters for pursuing him: "They signed him up illegally. He shouldn't have been signed up when they found out he had had a lifetime of asthma and mental problems to the point where he's got burns, he's got scars all over his arms. They never should have signed him up. That's not counting the drug problem he had in high school."

And then she says this: "I love my son. I hate him being away."

While Ryan waits for his refugee application to be ruled on by the Canadian government so he can get a job, he seeks signatures from Canadians on petitions supporting him and the other deserters who hope to stay in Canada. He's trotted out his Army clothes to add emphasis to his role when appealing to Canadians. "It's more casual now," he says about his uniform, "I cut the legs off of it and cut the sleeves out of it. I cut all the buttons off of it."

Regarding work, Ryan's ambitions are minimal. "I've always been doing warehouse work and driving forklift and I enjoy that. I'll probably try and get a job here doing forklift or just working in a warehouse. And I'm going to try and go to college, because from what I understand, college is a lot cheaper here. That's one of the reasons that a lot of soldiers join, for college."

In the service, Ryan says, his college dreams evaporated. "Soldiers don't get to go to college. We don't have time to go to college. We have to ask permission to go to college, we have to ask for time off to go to college and it doesn't work out. Unless you're going to be an officer, they don't let you go to college. When I found that out, I was kind of pissed off. I was upset to find out that it's completely unlikely that any of us go to college." Recruiters, he says, "tell you everything you want to hear and they know what you want to hear. If you ask about college they say, 'Yeah, you can go to college.' Do I get to go overseas? 'Yeah, you get to go overseas, you get to see whatever you want.' Yeah, anything you want. That's what it is."

I ask Ryan if he has a message for his recruiter.

"Are you going to put it in your book?"

"Absolutely," I tell him.

"I want to tell them that they're pieces of shit, and I don't think they should be telling eighteen-year-old kids all these lies, you know? Because someone gets right out of high school, you know, and never had a job before, they want to hear that everything's going to be easy and everything's going to be paid for – that's what people want to hear. When someone tells them something like that, they want to believe that it's the truth. So thousands of soldiers are believing it. I just want to go in there and just tell them to fuck off."

Outside the Visalia Army recruiting office, I found Sergeant Quick, the recruiter who got the credit for signing Ryan Johnson. She was in uniform, getting out of a sporty white car. I introduced myself with a hearty, "Hi, how are you?"

"I'm good, yourself?" She flashed a nice smile.

I told her that I was working the Ryan Johnson story, that I'm a journalist. "Do you remember Ryan Johnson?" I asked.

"Yes, I do," she started to look wary.

"Ryan is no longer in the military," I said.

"That's correct," she agreed.

"What happened with him?"

"I have no idea."

"I spoke with him up in Canada," I told her. "It seems that it didn't work out with him and the military. He's making a new life for himself up there. One of the things he told me that I wanted to check with you about was that when you were recruiting him you said things to him that he felt were not straight."

"That's not true." She was firm in her response. I was following her now as she walked toward the recruiting station. "His mom was here, and everything that I said to him he found to be true. I don't know what Ryan's telling you, but I have nothing further to say." She was no longer interested in a chat.

"He said that, among other things, you said to him that he wouldn't be going to Iraq."

"Like I said, I don't know what Ryan is telling you, but that's not what I told him. And he knows it." Her tone was antagonistic now, and defensive at the same time.

At this point Sergeant Quick retreated to her desk – the screen saver on her computer showed the New York skyline with the memorial twin beams of light shining up from where the Twin Towers used to stand – and her superior placed himself between us and invited me into his office. I asked him about Ryan's charges and he placed a call, using his speakerphone, to First Sergeant Paul Senn, the man charged with supervising all the recruiting stations in the San Joaquin Valley.

I told him about Ryan's charges of lies and broken promises.

"We cannot respond to any of that, sir," said the sergeant. "The thing is, that's not standard procedures for the United States Army. We don't lie, cheat, or steal. You know? The small incidences that happened out in Colorado" – he was referring to recruiters who were caught instructing potential recruits in techniques for cheating drug tests and faking high school transcripts – "I can't make comments on that. All we see is negative press. That's one of the reasons we don't respond to anybody." But respond he did. "We've never had any good positive press anywhere. Nobody strives on positive press because that doesn't sell, but negative press sells. You know what I mean?"

Before he hung up, Sergeant Senn not only insisted that the Army doesn't lie, cheat, or steal, he questioned the credibility of Ryan's charges because Ryan was a deserter. He spat out the word "deserter" with disgust.

Ryan is unwilling to consider a return to America and prison time. "It seems absolutely insane," he says. "They'll put someone in jail for five years for not wanting to kill somebody. I'm trying to avoid killing people. I know if I went to Iraq I would kill somebody. If I got put on patrol I would probably shoot somebody, because I would know that it's them or me, you know? And they feel the same way. If I don't kill these guys they're going to kill me."

An American without a country is how Ryan identifies his nationality now. "I consider myself an American because I believe in free speech and I believe in all the general rights that a person should have: the right to live, the right to be happy, things like that."

Ryan acknowledges that when he first went AWOL it was for selfish survival reasons. Now, he says, he's been politicized. "I want people to know why people are going AWOL. I want people to know how many people are going AWOL. I want people to know how many people are dying. I characterize myself as just a guy that made a wrong decision who wants a forklift job. And I'm an activist. And an AWOL soldier. I can't get a job right now, so right now, I'm mostly an activist. I'm fighting for the things that the United States was founded on, you know? The United States wasn't founded on oil. It wasn't founded on the fact that everyone has the right to lay a pipeline in Afghanistan. It wasn't founded on the fact that some guy can make money from Halliburton building things in Iraq."

Ryan is hoping to feel at home in Canada, despite

the fact that it appears to him oddly similar to the United States. His introduction to the new country when he drove across the border was unexpectedly welcoming. He says he tried to give his ID to the border guard, but she was not interested in checking it. She just said, "Welcome to Canada." He and Jennifer were surprised with the easy crossing.

"Yeah, that's what she said. She said, 'Welcome to Canada.' And I said, 'Thank you!' and then we crossed the border and Jennifer screamed."

★ 4 ★
THE DESERTERS' ADVOCATES

Ryan Johnson is convinced the Canadian government will grant him refugee status and that he will be able to start a new life. Maybe, maybe not.

Canada is proud of its long history as a refuge for escapees coming north, from loyalists to King George during the American Revolution, to slaves who traveled up on the Underground Railroad, to Vietnam War deserters and draft dodgers. When the Vietnam-era migration first started, Canada balked. Codifying what had been unwritten policy, the immigration authorities implemented Operational Memorandum No. 117 in 1966: "Officers will not refuse an immigrant solely on the grounds that he is known to be, or suspected of being, a draft evader." But it was unequivocal on deserters, ordering that a soldier "will not be issued a visa or granted admission until he has submitted proof of his discharge."[16]

After a couple of years of heated debate about the issue in Canada, coupled with growing traffic of draft dodgers and deserters at border crossings, the liberal Pierre Trudeau was elected prime minister in 1968. Initially his government continued to bar deserters from immigrating. During a March 1969 trip to Washington to meet with newly elected President Richard Nixon, Trudeau spoke to the National Press

Club and acknowledged the imbalance in U.S.-Canadian relations, comparing the Canadian position to "sleeping with an elephant. No matter how friendly and even-tempered the beast, if I can call it that, one is affected by every twitch and grunt."

Nonetheless, just two months later, Trudeau opened the border to those wishing to escape the U.S. military, and ultimately tens of thousands of Americans changed their addresses and often their citizenship rather than fight in the Vietnam War. Canada remains most pleased with its policy, as evidenced by the statement on the website of Citizenship and Immigration Canada (CIC): "Although some of these transplanted Americans returned home after the Vietnam War, most of them put down roots in Canada, making up the largest, best-educated group [of immigrants] this country had ever received."

Yet the arrival of Iraq War soldiers seeking refuge in Canada didn't sit well with officials. Army Specialist Jeremy Hinzman's case was the first to be adjudicated, after he became the first U.S. war resister ever to apply for refugee status in Canada. The Immigration and Refugee Board denied his claim; appeals may drag on for years. While his case is pending, Canada allows him to stay in the country and provides him with a temporary work permit. The ruling from the Refugee Protection Division of CIC insists Hinzman failed to make a case that the Iraq War was illegal: "He has not shown that the U.S. has, either as a matter of deliberate policy or official indifference, required or allowed its combatants to engage in widespread actions in violation of humanitarian law." [17]

A veteran of the U.S. action in Afghanistan, Hinzman took his wife and baby to Canada when he received his orders at Fort Bragg for a tour of duty in Iraq. "No matter how much I wanted to, I could not convince myself that killing someone was right," he said once he surfaced in Toronto.[18] Hinzman had applied to be discharged as a conscientious objector, requested noncombat duties, and spent much of his time in Afghanistan performing kitchen chores. His CO application was rejected after a hearing in Afghanistan. Back in the States, when his orders for Iraq came, Hinzman felt he had only two choices: disobey them and risk prison, or flee the country.

Prison was not an option. "I have already missed a large chunk of my young son's life and I wasn't willing to sacrifice any more lost time with him, especially during his formative years," he said. Canada looked like a good bet, given its policies toward deserters during the Vietnam War. Hinzman expressed no regrets about his decision and is convinced the Iraq War is illegal.

"I object to the Iraqi war," he announced, "because it is an act of aggression with no defensive basis. It has been supported by pretenses that cannot withstand even elementary scrutiny. First, before the U.S. dropped the first bomb, it was quite evident that Iraq had no weapons of mass destruction. Second, the Bush administration had the gall to exploit the American public's fear of terrorists by making the absurd assertion that a secular Baathist government was working with a fundamentalist terrorist group. There was never any intelligence to substantiate this. Third, the notion that the U.S. wants to export democracy to Iraq is laughable. Democracy is by the people, not an appointed puppet theater."[19]

Once Hinzman went public, the reaction from Canadians was both positive and negative. Some pundits accused him of cowardice. "While good manners dictate that no one wants to come out and say it, it's hard to escape the conclusion that Jeremy Hinzman is a coward," wrote Peter Worthington in the March 28, 2005, edition of the *Toronto Sun*. "These guys are deserters, and there's a certain disdain for deserters. Even during Vietnam, a draft dodger was more acceptable than a deserter, which reeks of cowardice no matter how one sugarcoats it. Hinzman will be an antiwar hero to those aging anti-Vietniks who came here 30 to 40 years ago. But mostly he is a sad young man whose judgment is flawed and whose courage is questioned."

It's worth noting that Hinzman has a close personal connection to the Vietnam War: His wife, Nga Nguyen, was born in Laos in 1972 – the last year Americans were at war with Vietnam – and arrived at a refugee camp in California after that war ended.

Barrister Jeffry House is representing Hinzman, Ryan Johnson, and other U.S. soldiers who have picked Canada as their exit strategy from military service. House is doing the work pro bono; the issue is close to his heart. While he was living in Wisconsin in

1970, his draft lottery number came up 16. The day he was ordered to report for induction, he left and settled in Canada. Now a criminal defense lawyer, he's argued plenty of refugee cases over the years and feels confident that eventually he'll win permanent immigrant status for his new American clients.

House and I meet for lunch at a crowded falafel joint across from a dreary criminal court building on the north side of Toronto. He tells me that when Hinzman came to his office looking for help, he saw himself as a young man. "I remember asking Jeremy, 'Why don't you want to serve in Iraq?' He said, 'Because it's bogus. The war is bogus, it's based on bogus principles.' And it really struck a chord with me because that's exactly how I felt about Vietnam." He looks at my gray beard and says, "You're old enough to know about the Tonkin Resolution and the Fulbright hearings and all that. I remember being outraged that they had lied basically about the character of the Gulf of Tonkin Resolution. So when Jeremy started giving me chapter and verse about no WMD, no connection to al-Qaeda, I was impressed and I felt, yeah – it's the same thing happening again. I felt a lot of affinity for him. I know there are differences but there sure are some similarities."

Not only does House oppose the Iraq War, he is disgusted that politicians who avoided fighting in past wars themselves launched it and are directing it. "I consider it an aggravating circumstance that basically the people who didn't participate in the antiwar movement in the sixties and seventies are the ones who are running this war, people who learned nothing then and now they're exposing young people to this war. They didn't learn anything. If you had an actual government based on people who learned something from the Vietnam War, you'd be in a much better position. But the government is those who didn't serve but didn't learn."

House is balding now, but there's still enough hair left for it to hang a little from the back of his head over the collar of his white shirt. Despite the summer heat wave, he's wearing a tie. As important as House finds the cases of the Americans he's defending, he sees a greater cause, the philosophy of his adopted nation. "We always quote Pierre Trudeau, who said Canada should be a refuge from militarism. He said that when he accepted fifty-five thousand Americans who were in the country at the time. There is a much bigger cause than just these twelve," he says about his clients.

Despite the hearty "Welcome to Canada" Ryan and Jennifer heard at the border, their lawyer is not sure they and the other deserters seeking refugee status in Canada will be allowed to stay, and he refrains from encouraging other Americans to escape north to avoid service in Iraq – despite the fact that he did just that to dodge the draft. "I believe that it is most likely that no one will go back, but I can't be absolutely certain, and I wouldn't want to say anything that would cause anyone to take an action that later on I'm responsible for."

The legal argument House is presenting is based on the Nuremberg principles, developed during the post–World War II trials of Nazis and then codified by the United Nations as what constitutes war crimes and crimes against humanity.[20] He contends that Hinzman and the other deserters came to Canada to avoid serving in an illegal war and are therefore obligated to reject orders to participate.

To convince the Canadian government to assert that U.S. policy violates international law seems a difficult challenge.

"U.S. policy is already indicted worldwide," House points out, "I figure it would be nice if a Canadian court said, 'Yes, this war is illegal.' But it's pretty clearly illegal whether they say so or not." Rather than making an official policy statement about the Iraq War by offering a blanket welcome to any U.S. soldier who wishes to come to Canada to avoid that war, House thinks the government may continue to approach each case individually.

We talk about the youth and relative naïveté of so many of the soldiers recruited for the Iraq War, soldiers who quickly realize they've been misled by recruiters and begin to question the Bush administration's policies in Iraq. House mentions Brandon Hughey, from San Angelo, Texas, just eighteen years old when he drove to Canada instead of deploying to Iraq.

"When I met him I said, 'Why don't we go out and have lunch and talk about this?'" House relates. "He said, 'That's great.' And I said, 'What would you like? Would you like to go get Chinese food? Indian food? You know, there's a great Thai place down the road.' And he said, 'Oh, I haven't really been to any of those places, I've only had steak and I've been to Mexico' –

because he's from West Texas, right? It doesn't prove anything, but it suggests he's sort of isolated."

During their lunch Brandon told House how he was seduced by recruiters with the promise of a signing bonus. "He said the recruiter called him on the phone and said, 'Brandon? Brandon, this is Staff Sergeant So-and-so down at the United States Army Recruiting and I've got a check here for you in your name in the amount of five thousand dollars. Would you like to come down and discuss it?' And Brandon said to me, 'Well, I knew my dad had some debts at that time, and I thought he was really a good dad to me and I thought I'd like to help him repay those debts. It was like at that moment I decided I'm going to act like a man, you know?'" House is disgusted as he finishes the story: "He signed up. He never got any bonus."

House tells me that while more than 50 percent of the Americans who chose Canada instead of the military during the Vietnam War were university graduates, none of his clients fleeing the Iraq War have college degrees. But there is no question that they are getting a specialized education since they deserted; they are being tutored by the War Resisters Support Campaign about U.S. history, Iraq and Middle Eastern history, the Vietnam War, and conscientious objection – all from a distinctly antiwar perspective. "Then they send them out on the road giving speeches," House reminds me. "And nothing is more calculated to get you to think seriously about what's happening, and what and who you are, and what's right and what's wrong, than having to explain it to four thousand people."

★★★

While Jeffry House works the refugee board and the courts, some members of the Canadian Parliament use their bully pulpits to try to persuade Canadians that welcoming the deserters is both the right thing to do and in Canada's best interests. One of those is Bill Siksay, who represents the eastern suburbs of Vancouver and specializes in immigration and civil rights issues. He believes the fact that a majority of Canadians "strongly" opposed the Iraq War means Canada should welcome war resisters fleeing the United States. He tells me that if the deserters are not granted refugee status as individuals, the government should offer a sweeping plan that simply allows them to come north and settle "much like what was done for draft dodgers during the Vietnam War." This could be done, he believes, with an executive order signed by the minister of the Citizenship and Immigration department. Legislation to regularize the status of the deserters would take a long time to come to a vote, and whether it would pass Parliament, of course, is an unknown. But he's confident many Canadians support the deserters: "I think there is a fairly significant and broad group of Canadians who want to be supportive of these people making this stand for conscience, and I'm happy to be standing with them.

"I want members of the armed forces to be thinking, conscientious folks – to consider the impact of their actions," he adds. "I can understand how somebody's understanding of their service may change as circumstances change. I can understand how someone may have enlisted for other reasons and be confronted with the situation in Iraq, or may have had a tour of duty in Iraq and because of that experience may come back with a different understanding of involvement there. I want to be supportive of those who, for solid conscientious reasons, come to a different position on the war and a different position on their participation in the armed forces."

I remind Siksay that the American immigrants dodging the draft were often highly educated and provided Canada with the opposite of a brain drain, while the Iraq War deserters are often undereducated. "I think someone of conscience is always an asset to Canada," he responds. "People who think clearly about the important issues of the day, think clearly about their involvement in world affairs and their involvement in social change, are always an asset to Canada. I have no concerns about the current group."

The American deserters meet with supporters on a regular basis, meetings their lawyer attends. "They talk and they plan and then they all go out drinking and they have debates about everything," says Jeffry House. Drinks are often at a funky saloon called Goodman's, a hangout in the 1960s and 1970s for Vietnam War deserters and draft dodgers. "And it's good. If you never thought about anything and you're now being asked, 'What's the status of the Israeli occupation of Palestine, of the West Bank, as opposed to the American occupation of Iraq. . . .'" House muses about the immersion classes in world affairs the deserters' new lifestyle creates, and he's pleased that these unsophisticated young men are being exposed to new intellectual opportunities – and taking advantage of them.

"The only one I would exempt is Jeremy, who was amazingly sophisticated; he's a bit older – he's twenty-five – he's amazingly sophisticated," says House, and proceeds to relate a story about Hinzman. "Guys came from Norway to interview him. He met them and he immediately started talking to them about Knut Hamsun [Norway's infamous Nazi sympathizer and Nobel Prize–winning writer], saying, 'You guys are from Norway, so what do you think about his book *Hunger*? Do you think that it was a progressive book?' They had read *Hunger* because you have to read your own literature. But that's pretty impressive."

Before House heads from our lunch back to the courthouse, he tells me the story of one more war resister he's heard about who is seeking refuge in Canada from the U.S. military. At first I think he's joking when he says, "He's a Tutsi born in Rwanda and he's in Windsor."

A Tutsi born in Rwanda living in Windsor, Ontario, and seeking asylum in Canada from the U.S. military?

"Yeah," says House casually. He clearly loves the seeming non sequitur. "He was born in Rwanda. He was ten or eleven years old at the time of the massacre. He lost two hundred members of his family. Slaughtered. He saw their guts, you know. Somehow he was allowed to come to the United States with his uncle. He said he felt so grateful to the United States that he always felt that he would do something for them at the first opportunity. When he was allowed to sign up, he did. He got into basic training and he said all of a sudden all of these memories started flooding back. They used to do bayonet practice, and he had seen his family just brutally slaughtered. [Most of the Rwandan murders were by long knives.] He said he started to think about it and he couldn't do it. He couldn't do it and he was throwing up. They're only working on dummies during bayonet training. He went to his superior and his superior didn't know anything about Rwanda, didn't care anything about Rwanda, and said, 'Well, you'll get over it. Everybody is a little queasy at first.' He ended up in Windsor, where he's got a lawyer helping him. But that's a very affecting story, the fact that they weren't willing to help him."

As we say good-bye, House contemplates the raw anger he felt during the Vietnam War, how the news of the Tiger Cages, the Phoenix Program, the napalming, and the My Lai massacre made him feel crazy. After living through such a period, he says, "It's impossible to be a moral being and not freak out." Why, he wonders, is there so little happening in America against the Iraq War?

In the same downtown Toronto hipster neighborhood where many of the Vietnam War draft dodgers and deserters made their Canadian landfall in the 1960s and 1970s, the War Resisters Support Campaign occupies a modest donated space in the United

Steelworkers building,[21] a squat glass-and-steel warren of offices with a view east toward the Toronto skyline. T-shirts and buttons are for sale, emblazoned with the declaration WAR RESISTERS WELCOME HERE and decorated with the silhouette of a soldier walking away from his discarded rifle. Clippings are posted from newspapers: "War Resisters Rescue American GIs Hiding in Canada" and "U.S. War Resister Publicizes His Plight at Peace Forum."

Lee Zaslofski answers the phone with a businesslike "War Resisters" when it rings. It's a hot summer day and he's wearing a T-shirt, shorts, and tennis shoes with white socks. His hair is close-cropped and complements his short goatee and moustache. Zaslofski is a Vietnam War deserter who came to Canada in 1970 and is now a Canadian citizen. "I consider myself Canadian, not American," he says. Now he counsels and lobbies, demonstrates and speaks, raises money and collects signatures – all in support of this new surge of incoming American soldiers.

We talk about the differences between deserters from the volunteer Army fighting the Iraq War and those, like Zaslofski, who were drafted to fight in Vietnam. Members of his generation, he points out, were politicized, supported by a large peace movement, and highly educated, since they had used student deferments to stay out of the Army. Most Iraq War soldiers, he's convinced, "are recruited on the basis that there is money to be made, there is college education to be had, there's skills training and free medical care. That's a big deal for someone like Joshua Key. He had three kids at the time he enlisted."

Zaslofski is impressed that the deserters he's working with made their choice to flee the Army without the support groups Vietnam-era soldiers and draftees found on university campuses and within the peace movement. "They came to their decision pretty much on an individual basis, on a personal basis, rather than feeling that they were part of a larger movement that was opposed to the war." Those singular decisions make deserters easy targets for the critics who charge them with cowardice. Nonsense, says Zaslofski. "That's what you always say when you want someone to stay in the Army, that they're cowards if they leave. That's how they keep people in. Shame. That's how it works."

The War Resisters office is like a social club for the deserters, providing not only logistical support for their petitions to stay in Canada, but also a community crossroads for them as they adapt to their new homeland, their sanctuary from war. The atmosphere at the meeting I attend goes back and forth between serious political organizing and fraternity house banter.

A young man named Ivan plays with his skateboard. Another, named Cliff, suggests Ivan will lose control of his board and wreck stuff in the office.

"I'm going to throw you out the window," Cliff says to Ivan.

He gets a boyish grin back from Ivan, who admonishes him with, "That's an unnecessary escalation of force."

When Ivan leaves the room to prop open the front door for late-coming meeting participants, Cliff hides his skateboard.

Another young man, Darrell Anderson, fiddles with his pocket watch, which has a Canadian flag on its face. He's wearing a peace symbol necklace. Ryan Johnson's T-shirt reads CALIFORNIA HOTEL.

Volunteer Michelle Robidoux is in charge of the meeting. "We're going to be getting a sofa," she announces. The organization survives on donations, and Michelle reports on the latest offerings: The Catholic Worker house, where Ryan and Jennifer live, is opening more rooms for deserters. Two Canadians in London, Ontario, are offering housing. News of a fresh arrival in Vancouver, some two thousand miles away on Canada's west coast, is greeted with delight.

"That would be number sixteen!"

"Wow, that's great!"

Cliff is reminded to resubmit his work permit application. He forgot to sign it when he first sent it to the authorities.

"Forgot to sign this?" Ivan holds the form up in front of Cliff and, with a big smile, teases him and reads to him the instruction to sign the form. "It says it in big bold letters," reports Ivan to the group.

Cliff gives Ivan a deadpan look and a middle finger.

The group discusses spreading the word to homeless shelters around Canada that if deserters show up for help they should be referred to the Campaign. Michelle leads a short discussion about the Bush speech the night before at Fort Bragg, another attempt at cheerleading for the troops. There is a reminder of Joshua and Brandi's upcoming cross-Canada speaking tour.

The deserters are not alone. They've created a community for themselves, midwifed with sophistication by their Canadian advocates.

"There is a historic echo," Michelle Robidoux tells me at a coffeehouse just down the street from the War Resisters office. "My neighbors when I was growing up were these young war resisters. The fact that they were exiled because of the war in Vietnam, that left an imprint on lots and lots of people in this country. We have a history and a responsibility to keep that option open for people. We have to make sure that they are not kicked out." She reminds me that Canada refused to join the U.S. invasion of Iraq. "If Canada is going to kick people out who refuse to participate in the war, Canada might as well have sent soldiers."

Robidoux dismisses the distinction between the draft-fueled Vietnam-era Army and the volunteer Army serving in Iraq, questioning – as do many observers – whether the Army serving in Iraq is genuinely volunteer. She suggests that young Americans are compelled to join the Army because of an "economic draft" and a "poverty draft," that "stop-loss" [22] and other small print in the enlistment contract means, "Even if you're finished, you're not finished." The net effect, she says, is not much different than conscription.

No deserter from the U.S. military has faced a

firing squad since World War II.[23] But some opponents of the Iraq War who refused to return to Iraq for more duty (or to go in the first place) and instead stayed in the United States to face charges have been sentenced to substantial prison time. Sergeant Kevin Benderman received a fifteen-month sentence after he followed a tour of duty in Iraq with an application for conscientious objector status. After six months in combat in Iraq, Sergeant Camilo Mejía was sentenced to a year behind bars for refusing to return to the war theater. Lance Corporal Stephen Funk drew a six-month sentence for refusing to obey orders to deploy to Iraq.

Robidoux considers the prison penalty substantial and worth avoiding. Canada, in her opinion, is a much better alternative. "Why would you accept to spend a day in jail for basically upholding international law?" she asks. Moving to Canada, she points out, allows soldiers to get on with their lives.

"I can't get over how young these guys are," Robidoux shakes her head, "and stuck in this situation. I'm just glad more of them are coming. They can help each other."

Brandon Hughey was just eighteen when he crossed the border. He roomed with Robidoux for several months after he first arrived in Toronto. She reports that the Texan adjusted fine to Canada with the exception of missing his Fluffernutter. She finally managed to get a jar of Fluff-brand marshmallow spread sent to him so that he could make himself a sandwich out of the marshmallow and peanut butter mixture.

"Did you try it?" I ask her.

"No, I'm too old for that," she insists, the beginnings of a smile creeping onto her serious face.

Robidoux's agenda is not limited to helping the deserters. "Iraq is where the U.S. has to be defeated – categorically defeated," she tells me. "We have to impose the kind of limit on the U.S. ability to conduct mayhem around the world that was imposed by the Vietnam defeat. There's only a few ways that can happen. There has to be a refusal within the military to participate, and obviously there has to be a refusal around the world to support it."

Darrell Anderson joined the Army just before the Iraq War started, motivated by a common litany of immediate worries. "I needed health care, money to go to college, and I needed to take care of my daughter. The military was the only way I could do it," he tells me as we chat outside the United Steelworkers building, basking in the sun on a peaceful Toronto street. After fighting for seven months in Iraq, he came home bloodied from combat, with the Purple Heart that proved his sacrifice – and seriously opened his eyes. "When I joined I wanted to fight. I wanted to see combat. I wanted to be a hero. I wanted to save people. I wanted to protect my country."

But soon after he arrived in Iraq, he tells me, he realized the Iraqis did not want him there, and he heard harsh tales that surprised and distressed him. "Soldiers were describing to me how they had beaten prisoners to death," he says. "There were three guys and one said, 'I kicked him from this side of the head while the other guy kicked him in the head and the other guy punched him, and he just died.' People I knew. They were boasting about it, about how they had beaten people to death." He says it again: "Boasting about how they had beaten people to death. Because they are trained killers now. Their friends had died in Iraq. So they weren't the people they were when before they went there."

Darrell says even the small talk in his unit was difficult to tolerate. "I hate Iraqis," he quotes his peers saying. "I hate these damn Muslims." At first he was puzzled by such talk. "After a while I started to understand. I started to feel the hatred myself. My friends were dying. What am I here for? We went to fight for our country, now we're just fighting to stay alive." In addition to taking shrapnel from a roadside bomb – the injury that earned him a Purple Heart – Darrell says he often found himself in firefights.

But it was work at a checkpoint that made him seriously question his role. "I was guarding the backside" of a street checkpoint in Baghdad, he says. If a car passed a certain point without stopping, the guards were supposed to open fire. "A car comes through and it stops in front of my position. Sparks are coming from the car from bad brakes. All the soldiers are yelling. It's in my vicinity, so it's my responsibility. I didn't fire. My superiors go, 'Why didn't you fire? You were supposed to fire.' I said, 'It was a family!' At this time it had stopped. You could see the children in the back seat. I said, 'I did the right thing.' He's like, 'No, you didn't. It's procedure to fire. If you don't do it next time, you're punished.'"

Darrell shakes his head at the memory. "I'm already not agreeing with this war. I'm not going to kill innocent people. I can't kill kids. That's not the way I was raised." He says he started to look around at the ruined cityscape and the injured Iraqis – and began to understand the Iraqi response. "If someone did this to my street, I would pick up a weapon and fight. I can't kill these people. They're not terrorists. They're fourteen-year-old boys, they're old men. We're occupying the streets. We raid houses. We grab people. We send them off to Abu Ghraib, where they're tortured. These are innocent people. We stop cars. We hinder everyday life. If I did this in the States, I'd be thrown in prison." He recounts the house raids he conducted. "We drug men out. Women were crying. Just off a tip from some drunken Iraqi that stumbled into our base and said, 'They're over there,' we raid a house. We were just taking innocent people and sending them off to prison because we had a tip they might be planning to attack us."

Darrell describes another Baghdad street battle that scarred him – and scared him about himself. He was in an armored vehicle, with other soldiers riding on the outside, when it came under attack from rocket-propelled grenades. One of the soldiers riding outside was hit. "He free-falls. Drops his weapon and falls into the vehicle." Darrell says the scene still returns to him in his nightmares every night. "I look at him and he is bleeding everywhere. He's spitting up blood."

Someone has to take his place on the outside, Darrell realizes. "Me, I'm gung ho. I go up there. There're explosions. They tell us if you're under attack, you open fire on anybody in the streets. They say they're no longer innocent if they're there. I take my weapon and I find someone running. I point and I pull my trigger, but my weapon is still on safe." By the time he clicked it over to fire, Darrell says, he realized he was about to shoot a kid who was running away from the violence, a kid he was sure was not part of the battle. More traumatic, he says, were his own emotions. "I'm angry. My buddy is dying. I just want to kill." He says he realized then that he had become a different man, changed by the pathology of war and the suffering of the innocents. "When I first got there, I was disgusted with my fellow soldiers. But now I'm just the same. I will kill innocent people, because I'm not the person I was when I got there." The attack ebbed and Darrell survived it, as did the running boy.

Birds are singing sweetly as we talk, the contrast stark against Darrell's matter-of-fact delivery about atrocities in Iraq. "I didn't shoot anybody when I was in Baghdad. We went down to Najaf with howitzers [mobile field artillery]. We shot rounds in Najaf and we killed hundreds of people. I did kill hundreds of people, but not directly hand-to-hand."

Darrell went home for Christmas, convinced he would be sent back to the war. He knew he would not be able to live with himself if he returned to Iraq, armed with his first-hand knowledge of what was occurring there day after day. He decided he could not again participate, and his parents – already antiwar themselves – supported his decision. Canada seemed like the best option. After Christmas 2004, he drove from Kentucky to Toronto. "I'll never regret coming to Canada." Darrell Anderson feels as if he's finally found his calling: lecturing to whomever will listen about the evils of the Iraq War, hoping to help bring it to an end.

While Brandon Hughey waited for the Canadian government to decide his fate, his father, David Hughey, walked up to a microphone in Texas in a hall full of Iraq War opponents gathered at the Veterans for Peace conference.

"I'm the father of Private Brandon Hughey," he told the audience, which broke into prolonged applause before he added, "who is at this time in Canada." With a slow drawl, he proceeded to tell his story.

"I'm basically a card-carrying Republican." He paused. "Used to be." More applause and laughter.

"My story basically began when my young son called me from Canada and told me that he didn't want to risk his life for Bush and Cheney's son." Hughey interrupted the renewed applause to push on. "That caused me a great deal of concern. As a matter of fact, it caused great conflicts. Our first several conversations over the telephone were basically fights." Hughey paused again to compose himself. "But I started reading. I did a lot of research, an incredible amount of research. And I actually found myself not being able to believe what I was seeing happen to this country. So I sent my son basically a manifesto that said I support him. It took a lot out of me." Another emotion-laden pause before he added: "As I guess you can tell, I'm not much of a speaker."

A yell came from the audience, "You're doing all right!" And the hall again filled with applause.

"So it's brought me to this point, basically, to make a long story short," Hughey continued. "You know, I've read the Constitution of the United States of America. I've read a lot of books written by a man named James Madison, a lot of things by Thomas Jefferson. When I did that, it helped me figure out that all of this is totally wrong." Another pause. "I had some really good quotes, but I can't recall 'em off the top of my head." The tension was broken with more laughter.

"I just thought I'd come up and introduce myself. I do support my son." He hesitated, and then added to loud, loud applause, "I guess I should quit while I'm ahead."

★ 5 ★
CLARA GOMEZ
A Great Escape

Clara Gomez was not looking for a career in the Army. In late 2003, the seventeen-year-old student at Watsonville High School, south of Santa Cruz, California, was busy keeping her grade point average at 3.8 and considering universities. One day, the telephone rang at her home and an Army recruiter, Sergeant Daniel Lopez, was on the line.

"He called me and said he wanted to go to my house and meet my parents. I'd never heard of him. I never called the Army. He called me," says Clara. We're at a Starbucks, next to the Target in a shopping center near downtown Watsonville, a market town with a large Latino population in the midst of a prime strawberry-growing region about half an hour's drive south of Santa Cruz.

Clara's hair is pulled back tight, she's wearing a blue sweatshirt with jeans, and she jumps into her story needing little prompting. She says she later attributed the surprise phone call from the recruiter to a school chum who had suggested to Sergeant Lopez that Clara might be susceptible to his sales pitch.

"He acted as if he knew me; he's like, 'Oh, hi! How're you doing?' I was trying to place him somewhere. Then he introduced himself and said he wanted to go to my house. And talk to my parents."

Clara arranged a date for the recruiter to come to her house. Why not? He was convincing and she was curious. "I was a senior. I wanted a path. I was nervous about going to college. I wanted more choices." The Army's offer of money for college was seductive; the promise of adventure was luring. When he came to her home, Sergeant Lopez pulled out his laptop and showed her photographs of recruits parachuting and rock climbing. Clara's parents were not impressed, but told Clara they would support her if she chose the Army.

Soon after the home visit, the sergeant showed up after school at Watsonville High to take Clara for an aptitude test. In the car he introduced her to Christina, another potential recruit. After the test, Sergeant Lopez cheered Clara's results, telling her she qualified for training as a practical nurse. On his next visit to her home, he thrust a stack of papers at Clara's mother for her signature. Clara was still underage, so the Army needed parental permission to conduct the physical and induct her into the service. The papers were in English, which Clara's mother does not read or speak. She signed them nonetheless. A few days later Sergeant Lopez showed up again, this time to take Clara and Christina for a physical at an Army post in San Jose, an hour's drive north.

Clara's words are coming out faster now. "Why were we so naïve?" she asks. "We thought it was just a physical." But in San Jose, she was presented with another piece of official paper. "It said, 'If you want to enlist in the Army, check this box.'" Clara did not want to check the box; she had no intention of enlisting in the Army that day. She thought she was still checking it out. "What did I get myself into? Everybody in uniform. Everybody with a serious face. It's scary. Christina was also scared." As she tells me the story, she reverts to the present tense, as if she were back in San Jose. "What are we going to do now? Now we have to do everything they say." She was tested for drugs. Her eyes were tested. "'Christina, what are we going to do? He never told us we were going to sign any papers today.'"

When Clara next saw Sergeant Lopez, she confronted him. "I told him, 'Why did you bring me here? Why didn't you even tell me that I was supposed to sign something today?' He said, 'If I had told you, would you have come?' I said, 'No!' He's like, 'That's why I didn't tell you.' I was just so mad."

At that point she was called for another interview, in which she was asked by another recruiter what she thought about a job as a practical nurse. When she said it sounded interesting, "He handed me the papers. I'm like, 'No, no, no. Wait a minute. I have to sign something?' And he's like, 'Yeah, why do you think you're here?' His voice just totally changed with me. Sergeant Lopez was right there and I was looking at him, like, 'Help me out.' He didn't say anything." She says the other recruiter ordered Sergeant Lopez to take Clara out of the room and talk her into signing. "I kept telling him, 'I don't want to go, I don't want to go.'"

The words are coming in heated bursts now. She starts to cry. "This gets me so upset." She lifts her glasses and wipes her eyes and looks outside, reliving that day more than a year earlier. Then she continues to tell the tale, through tears and sniffles, twisting the strings of the hood of her sweatshirt back and forth. She seems even younger than the seventeen years old she had been when the Army came after her. "I told him my mom doesn't know anything about this. He said, 'Okay, we can fix that. There's a phone right over there.' I called my mom but I didn't want to upset her, and I just told her, 'Mom, this is going on.' I didn't want to sound worried. And she said, 'Well, if you want to, go ahead and do it.'" The tears keep flowing. "She wasn't happy with me going into the Army, but she was going to give me her support. I still had the papers in my hand, but I wasn't ready to do anything. I was thinking, 'I need to get out of here.'"

But she had no transport. Sergeant Lopez had driven her to San Jose. "I was just sitting there alone, just thinking, 'I'm scared.' The guy called me again and I said, 'No! I don't want to, I don't want to!' And he got upset and he took me to some other person, I think of a higher rank. He was nice, he was smiling, and he started saying how good the hospital I would be working at was. He kept saying that it was a very good opportunity, and how could I say no to it? He just gave me the pen. I had the pen in my hand now, so all I did was just sign it."

Clara takes a breath. I ask her why she signed it.

"I just wanted it to end." The tears subside. "The second person I spoke to, he made everything seem fine. 'You're going to be doing this for your country. It's going to be great. You're going to have fun working with these people.' I was like, 'Maybe he's right.' That morning I got up around four. It was late now. All the testing and stuff, I was tired. I just wanted out."

But the ordeal was not over. There were fingerprints to be taken and more papers to be signed, such as the form designating an heir for Clara's last paycheck if she gave her life for the Army. "That's where I was like, 'I don't want this.'"

Her photograph was taken, and Clara received her United States Army Delayed Entry and Delayed Training Program ID card, complete with her name and rank. She was now Private Clara L. Gomez. She pulls the card out to show me. "I kept it to remind myself that I have to be careful when I sign papers." The reverse side is festooned with announcements in capital letters, the first line in quotes:

"I AM A PROUD SOLDIER IN AMERICA'S ARMY"

I WILL SUPPORT AND DEFEND THE CONSTITUTION OF THE UNITED STATES.

I WILL OBEY THE ORDERS OF THOSE APPOINTED OVER ME.

I WILL REFER MY CLASSMATES, FAMILY MEMBERS AND FRIENDS (RECRUITABLE AGE) TO MY RECRUITER, WHICH MAY HELP ME EARN A PROMOTION PRIOR TO LEAVING FOR BASIC TRAINING.

I WILL APPLY FOR PARTICIPATION IN THE HOMETOWN RECRUITER ASSISTANCE PROGRAM, WHICH COULD ALLOW ME TO RETURN TO MY HOMETOWN (NON-CHARGEABLE ABSENCE) AFTER AIT AND ASSIST MY RECRUITER FOR UP TO 16 DAYS.

MY GOAL IS TO BETTER MYSELF AND TO ALWAYS STRIVE TO BE ALL I CAN BE!!!

(AIT refers to "advanced individual training.")

Clara was finished for the day and Sergeant Lopez was a happy man. "He's like, 'Okay, now you're part of the family, blah, blah, blah.' And he hugged me," she says. "I was like, 'Okay, you got what you wanted.' Then he brought me home. In the car he told me how much fun it was going to be. I was mad at him. He never told me what was going to go on there." She breaks down again for a moment and shivers, her voice shaking, as she recounts how she and Christina had made a pact not to sign anything in San Jose.

In the days that followed, she didn't sleep or eat well. And she couldn't compare notes with Christina because Sergeant Lopez refused to give Clara her phone number, explaining that Christina could be a bad influence. "I thought I was never going to see her again," says Clara. "But then I saw her here at Target." It was Christina who told Clara that she could refuse to go to basic training, that she could renounce her status in the Delayed Entry Program. And it was Christina who had discovered the GI Rights Hotline and the new power that came with being connected with its volunteers. She was no longer alone in this swirling pressure and confusion. She had help.

Armed with new information about the reality of her obligations to the military, Clara wrote a no-nonsense letter to the recruiting office rejecting the Army. "My parents and I were coerced by Sergeant Lopez," she wrote. "The real reason why I ended up signing was because I was exhausted. I thought the only way to go home was by signing. I feel I was not in my five senses at the time and I feel that I was pushed to sign the contract."

She says she never heard from the Army after she sent the letter.

Her story told, her tears gone, Clara's voice gets firm. "I was scared. I was so mad at myself. How could I sign all those papers and be so naïve? And it did affect my life. It was my last semester and my goal was a 4.0. But then I couldn't think about anything else besides how to get out of the Army, so my GPA dropped to a 3.1. It still gets me mad, it gets me so mad." But her attitude is positive. "I try to get over it. I can tell people about it so it won't happen to them." She's beaming now, pleased with her victory over the system, proud of herself for standing up to the United States government. "Wow! When I think about it . . ." She smiles.

6

THE CONFLICTED RECRUITERS

Josh Sonnenfeld works hard to keep students like Clara Gomez informed about their rights in the face of aggressive military recruiters on school campuses. It was the No Child Left Behind Act – the federal law that mandated that public schools meet certain standards but did not provide the funds needed to accomplish those goals – that activated his response to the Iraq War and the military recruiting in his midst. Though surprisingly few Americans understood this when it went into effect, that law also requires local school districts to provide to military recruiters the names, home addresses, and home telephone numbers of all high school students approaching graduation and the minimum age for joining the service. Any school that fails to cough up these records faces loss of its federal funding, something few schools can afford to risk. A family can keep this information out of the hands of the recruiters, but only if it formally opts out of the law's requirements, which means the family must first be aware of this little-known provision of the law, then make a formal request that the school not share the records. Federal law also forces schools that allow college and job recruiters onto their campuses to welcome military recruiters.

"I thought it was ridiculous that our information could be given out to military recruiters without our permission," Josh tells me when we meet in a San Francisco café. He is a tall, gangling fellow, full of energy, now out of high school and studying at the University of California at Santa Cruz. "When they say students have the right to opt out, that's not really something that's going to protect students' privacy unless they notify students about it." But the law does not require such notification, and the number of parents who instruct schools to withhold contact information is minimal.[24]

Consequently, recruiters have all but unlimited access to high school students. They roam school hallways, show up at student dances and other social events, treat students to restaurant dinners,[25] and show off flashy clothing, cars, jewelry, and cash. (In addition to their regular pay and a housing allowance to live off base, recruiters receive special duty pay – spending money with which to treat and impress their targets.)[26] The message to students is clear: All this stuff can be yours if you join the military. It's a message that is especially appealing to students in the nation's poorer schools.

These attempts at student seduction were attacked in the *Wildcat* newspaper at University High School in Los Angeles, in a November 19, 2004, op-ed by student Jose Dubon. He complained about the massive recruiting budget and its intrusive tactics: "And with those billions of dollars, the Army managed to get a Hummer rolling on 24" dubs,[27] blasting rap, lined with flames on the side, outside of room C-161 with the Spanish words YO SOY EL ARMY[28] written on the sides of the massive vehicle." Dubon attacked the military for trying to take advantage of poor students. "Get militarism out of our schools," he wrote. "Do not allow students to be exposed to the recruiters' romanticized stories of one day having that Hummer, or happily traveling the world if they join the military. We do not need them in our place of learning."

Sonnenfeld had an unusual response when recruiters started showing up at his high school: He engaged in counterrecruiting, lobbying students against joining the military. "I was doing counterrecruiting because I started to learn about all the realities and all the truths behind military recruiting," he tells me. "I started to see what these recruiters were saying. They were talking about money for college and job training and traveling around the world, going to Hawaii and sitting on a beach and drinking a margarita. I started to learn all the statistics and to hear all the stories from veterans and people who had enlisted in the military about how that's not really the case. Most people don't get any college money." He pauses and smiles, "Not everybody gets to go to Hawaii, believe it or not!" Josh concedes that the recruiters are not necessarily lying, because some people do get the benefits that are held out as bait. But the promise of tuition money and job training is deceptive, he insists, since so few going through the system end up enjoying such benefits.

The idea behind counterrecruiting is to eliminate the manpower the government needs to prosecute war. The basic tool counterrecruiters use is proximity; Josh and his colleagues set up tables next to recruiters who show up on campus. They attempt to tell curious students another side of the story that the military is telling. They offer information about nonmilitary sources of college funding.

The counterrecruiters use the military's own paperwork to make their antiwar statement. Josh reads his peers the fine print in the enlistment agreement, which "says that anything can change at any time with or without notice to the enlistee. What that means is that recruiters can't make promises. If students knew this, they wouldn't believe everything that comes out of a recruiter's mouth."

The U.S. Armed Forces enlistment contract clearly states that every enlistee is susceptible to eight years of active duty, and that in the event of a war, enlistment automatically continues until six months after the war ends. It also says this: "Laws and regulations that govern military personnel may change without notice to me. Such changes may affect my status, pay, allowances, benefits, and responsibilities as a member of the Armed Forces REGARDLESS of the provisions of this enlistment/reenlistment document." [29]

Working virtually shoulder to shoulder alongside the recruiters, Josh came to realize that they're basically in the business of sales. "Recruiters are salesmen, are salesmen, are salesmen, are salesmen. Just like when you're buying anything, you need to check out the contract, you need to check out what the deal is. But they hate that word, they absolutely hate that word. They say, 'We're not salesmen,'" Josh imitates the deep, booming, authoritative voice of a sergeant.

Talking to the recruiters is an element of Josh's on-campus counterrecruiting tactics. "I would spend the whole lunch period talking to them so that they wouldn't be talking to anyone else." To his surprise, Josh found recruiters who opposed the war in Iraq, a mentality he finds incomprehensible.

Staff Sergeant Cody Wenner is a recruiter who seems to be against the Bush administration's Iraq policy – he said as much on a radio program that also featured Josh Sonnenfeld.[30] "Sometimes you have to put your personal feelings in the backseat and know that there is a greater cause," Wenner said. "I don't have to agree with it, but I have to do what my boss tells me to do. In four years I'll be retired and I'll be able to obviously expound on that and go into bigger detail." There was no face-to-face debate. The radio show host announced that the Marines refused to allow Sergeant Wenner to appear on a live microphone with Josh.

The radio exchange came just after the Army ceased recruiting for one day to make time for a highly publicized special training. It was a day for recruiters to "refocus our entire force" and remind them of "who we are as an institution," Major General Michael Rochelle, the commander of Army recruiting, told reporters at a Pentagon briefing. The military insists it requires its recruiters to practice appropriate and ethical behavior, but by mid-2005, having fallen far behind its manpower needs, the military was facing extensive charges of wrongdoing on the part of recruiters seeking to meet their ever-more-elusive quota of two new soldiers a month. Recruiters had falsified high school diplomas, offered to help potential recruits beat drug tests, and in one case threatened to arrest a man who refused to sign enlistment papers.[31] Sergeant Thomas Kelt was the desperate recruiter who left this message on Chris Monarch's answering machine: "Hey, Chris. This is Sergeant Kelt with the Army, man. I think we got disconnected. Okay, I know you were on your cell probably and just had a bad connection or something like that. I know you didn't hang up on me. Anyway, by federal law you got an appointment with me at two o'clock this afternoon at Greenspoint Mall, okay? That's the Greenspoint Mall Army Recruiting Station at two o'clock. You fail to appear and we'll have a warrant. Okay? So give me a call back."

Understandably worried, Monarch called back. He says he was told by Sergeant Kelt, "Oh, Chris. Don't worry about that. It's just a marketing technique I use." The tape was broadcast by Houston TV station KHOU. The Army's daylong "stand-down" for recruiters was announced the next day.

Less than two months later Kelt was promoted and made a supervisor at another recruiting office. The logic? Since Kelt had failed to follow recruiting guidelines, the Army explained, he was an ideal boss for other recruiters, since he knows the consequences of violating the Army's ethics codes.[32]

Sergeant Cody Wenner is a smooth-talking professional, and it showed as he answered questions from callers to the radio show. Rather than denying that such abuses take place, he minimized their importance, insisting they represent a few flawed recruiting sergeants, not an institutional mentality. "These individuals who were caught, they were willing to compromise themselves and their careers at any cost to get a contract." Wenner acknowledged the Marine Corps quota of two recruits a month per recruiter became more difficult as the Iraq War dragged on: "At the Marine Corps, we're struggling. We're doing what we can to make mission, but we are struggling. Times are getting tougher. The longer that the war goes on, obviously it has a big influence on the society about joining the Marine Corps."

At the time of the radio interview, five Marine recruits from the Santa Cruz office had been killed in action in Afghanistan or Iraq. "It breaks my heart," Wenner said about the deaths, but quickly added, "When I talk to somebody, they're making a conscious decision. They're making a very educated decision. They know as well as I do the repercussions it could have if they were to go somewhere. I never thought I would go over to the Middle East, and I've been there. It disturbs me to know that I'm signing them up, but I'm doing it for a better cause; it's not just for war. They're signing up to maybe better their life, have some better opportunities out there that they may not have had."

A caller named Ray suggested that the Iraq War was "illegal" and "based on lies" and asked Wenner what he thought about the war. "I have a hard time thinking this is for democracy when we're trashing our own democracy at home," Ray lectured the sergeant. The sergeant's reaction was surprisingly candid: "I'm going to tell you right now that some of that would be personal opinion that I would share with you. Unfortunately though, while we're over there in Iraq, that's a government policy and we've all elected our officials into office. It's one we would have to call our government on and say, 'Hey, why are we over there?' As a recruiter I can't answer that. I'm just a small piece of the puzzle. It would just be an opinionated answer, if that makes sense to you, Ray.

"I have my own reservations, but I have to support my boss," he continued, referring to President Bush. "It does bother me in my heart, but again, I have to do what my boss told me to do." There are other factors for Wenner besides his obligation to follow orders. He said he sees secure retirement just four years away, his financial responsibilities to his wife and kids, and a solid medical and dental plan as all mitigating his stated concerns about the war. "War is a fact of life," he said as he tried to explain his own role. "People are just never going to get along."

Josh Sonnenfeld holds out hope that Sergeant Cody Wenner may come over to his side. "Maybe at some point this guy is going to want to quit the military. Maybe at some point he's going to say, 'I just can't do this anymore.' That's happened."

One recruiter who became disgusted with the military's sales techniques prior to the Iraq War and eventually gave up his job is former Staff Sergeant Jimmy Massey, a twelve-year Marine Corps veteran and a founder of Iraq Veterans Against the War. Massey is full of stories from his recruiting days: stories about convincing prosecutors to get charges dismissed so that criminals would qualify for the service, about sweet-talking court clerks to make incriminating records disappear, about teaching recruits how to mask preexisting medical conditions – the kind that get one barred from the military. As part of his act to look cool for gullible teenagers, Massey said, he drove a fancy car, trying to convince potential recruits that the Marines offered financial independence. "I made sure I always dressed nice when I was off duty. You've got to play the part. Young kids are really materialistic minded." [33]

After three years chasing recruits, Massey said he was "tired of lying." He quit recruiting, but he reenlisted in the Marines just in time for the invasion of Iraq in March 2003.

"In one forty-eight-hour period," he told anyone who would listen once he returned to the States, "we killed over thirty civilians in vehicles that got past our roadblocks. We just lit them up with gunfire. But when we went to pull the charred corpses out of the cars we never found any weapons. They were just civilians."

Massey remembered the Iraqis at his checkpoints as being scared. "With the intelligence reports that we were given, it was very hard for us to distinguish the good guys from the bad guys. We ultimately started looking at everybody in Iraq as a potential suicide bomber or terrorist – from women to children to old men. We didn't know who the enemy was."[34]

One car that didn't stop when ordered to do so by Massey's unit was a red Kia Spectra with four occupants he cannot forget: "We fatally wounded three of them. We started pulling out the bodies, but they were dying pretty fast. The guy that was driving was just frickin' bawling, sitting on the highway. He looked at me and asked, 'Why did you kill my brother? He wasn't a terrorist. He didn't do anything to you.'" Massey says there was no contraband in the car. "The driver just ran around saying, 'Why? Why?' That's when I started to question."[35]

The Iraq assignment took its toll on the former recruiter. After complaining of depression and telling his superiors that the Corps was committing genocide, Massey was shipped back to the States and discharged. Reports had him walking around Asheville, North Carolina, where he used to recruit for the Marines, having traded in his flashy Mustang and recruiting propaganda for a sign that announced, I KILLED INNOCENT PEOPLE FOR OUR GOVERNMENT. Massey's stories from the war were published in France in a book he coauthored called *Kill! Kill! Kill!*[36]

More than a year after Massey hit the antiwar lecture circuit, his stories were contested by *St. Louis Post-Dispatch* reporter Ron Harris. "Each of his claims is either demonstrably false or exaggerated," Harris wrote on November 5, 2005, although he failed to prove them false or exaggerated in his news story. At best, he pointed out some inconsistencies in

Massey's accounts of sordid experiences in Iraq. Harris quoted several versions of the red Kia Spectra story that Massey (a victim of post-traumatic stress disorder) had told, and reported that there was no evidence that any of them occurred. The Pentagon also rejected Massey's claims, telling the *Washington Post*, "They've been looked into, and nothing has been substantiated." [37] It's telling that even the Defense Department doesn't call Massey a liar, but rather carefully calls his allegations unsubstantiated.

Harris's piece in the *Post-Dispatch* failed to mention that a year earlier Massey had harshly and publicly critiqued a news story filed by Harris when he was an embedded reporter traveling and living with Marines on their march into Baghdad. Harris insisted in an e-mail exchange with me that he was not retaliating for Massey's attack on his reporting. "I was not aware at all of any statements that Massey had made about me prior to yesterday, when it was mentioned to me by a writer for *Vanity Fair* and when you mentioned it now," Harris wrote to me on November 9, 2005. "As for the Kia incident, I spoke with Marines who were with Massey . . . and they don't recall any such incident. Nobody ever recalled an incident in which three civilians were killed in a shooting. They did recall incidents in which civilians were wounded in automobile shootings."

That two men recount incidents experienced in the notorious fog of war differently does not necessarily mean either is wrong. But more important, as the events detailed in this book plainly show, stories of ghastly events similar to those offered by Massey have been brought home from Iraq by a growing number of U.S. soldiers, especially about innocents injured or killed at checkpoints. America's role in Iraq has been thoroughly indicted by many more shocked eyewitnesses and candid perpetrators than just one Marine named Jimmy Massey.

William Branigin was an embedded *Washington Post* reporter with the Army's 3rd Infantry Division when soldiers – worried about potential suicide attacks on their checkpoint – hit a civilian Toyota, killing ten Iraqis, including five little children. In his April 1, 2003, story, Branigin quotes a grieving Army medic, Sergeant Mario Manzana, as saying it was "the most horrible thing I've ever seen, and I hope I never see it again."

Dexter Filkins, an embedded reporter for the *New York Times*, wrote on March 29, 2003, about a conversation with two 5th Marine Regiment sharpshooters who were fighting the Iraqi army during the initial American push to Baghdad. "We had a great day," he quotes Sergeant Eric Schrumpf. "We killed a lot of people." Schrumpf and his colleague, Corporal Mikael McIntosh, expressed frustration because some Iraqi soldiers were hiding among women and children. Both soldiers said they tried to avoid the bystanders but sometimes failed. Schrumpf described an incident in which his unit fired upon an Iraqi soldier standing next to civilians. A woman dropped to the ground, apparently shot dead. "I'm sorry," Sergeant Schrumpf said, "but the chick was in the way."

Soon after Ron Harris attempted to discredit Massey's Kia story, still another such tragedy occurred. Five members of an Iraqi family – unarmed – were killed on a street in Baquba, shot dead in their minivan near a U.S. base. Two of them were children. Four others were wounded. An Army gunner on a Humvee said he signaled the driver to stop, but when the car kept moving, he fired warning shots. Major Steve Warren, a spokesman for the Army's 3rd Infantry Division, explained what happened next: "This vehicle keeps coming at him, and he has literally an instant to decide. He knows his job is to protect himself and his buddies, and he knows that the terrorists put car bombs on the road every day. He followed the rules of engagement. What happened was a tragedy." Not so, said one of the grieving passengers in the minivan who managed to survive the attack. His sad version of events: "We were surprised by an American convoy and slowed down. As we tried to move over to let them pass, they opened fire." [38]

By September 2005, the Army was forced to acknowledge that, despite its aggressive recruiting campaign, it was going to miss its annual recruiting target, a shortfall that hadn't plagued the Army since 1999. The numbers were impressive: The regular Army was 80,000 recruits under its goal. Perhaps more telling of a change in the national attitude were the numbers for the Army National Guard and the Army Reserve. At the end of 2005, the National Guard – commanded by state governors until called up for active duty by the Defense Department – and the Army Reserve were contributing about 40 percent of the soldiers at work full-time in Iraq, even though these soldiers had joined the armed forces expecting to be part-time employees who would be pressed into a full-time role only in local emergency conditions like hurricanes or riots.

When the Pentagon tallied the final numbers for the fiscal year ending in September 2005, the National Guard was more than 20 percent under its recruiting quota, and the Reserve was just shy of 20 percent short. The 18,000-recruit shortfall in the National Guard and the Reserve combined with the Army's 80,000-recruit shortfall left the Army nearly 100,000 soldiers under its stated goal, and it readily admitted that the Iraq War was to blame. Neither an advertising blitz nor an announced increase in cash signing bonuses salvaged the year for the Army (the Marines, the Air Force, and the Navy all hit their recruiting targets).[39]

A 2005 qualitative analysis by the Government Accountability Office (GAO) – the nonpartisan investigative arm of Congress – found the military with inadequate expertise in its ranks to fill more than 40 percent of combat and noncombat jobs that require special training. These positions range from death-defying defusers of roadside bombs to intelligence analysts. The GAO report, issued on November 17, 2005, posed a critical question: "How can Department of Defense components continue to effectively execute their mission with consistently underfilled occupational specialties?" The GAO also questioned the effectiveness of the military's advertising blitz and the financial incentives offered to recruits and those who reenlist.

This failure took its toll on recruiters in the form of frustration, depression, and – from a military point of view – worse: In the period from late 2002 to early 2005, at least three dozen Army recruiters went AWOL.[40]

In July 2005 the Defense Department responded to the negative recruitment numbers by making a formal request that Congress raise the age limit for active-duty recruits from 35 to a rather astounding 42, calling it an "urgent wartime support initiative."[41]

Meanwhile, recruiters were pounding high school corridors, all but stalking students and those the military calls "influencers" – parents, teachers, and coaches. The Army created a special handbook for recruiters to help them interest students in the military and keep them interested until they leave high school and turn eighteen (or obtain parental consent to join the service as a minor). "Deliver donuts and coffee for the faculty once a month," the handbook instructs. "Get involved with local Boy Scout troops," "offer to be a timekeeper at football games," and "eat lunch in the school cafeteria several times a month." Recruiters are advised to keep the pressure on once students enroll in college. The language of the handbook is pragmatic but smells of overt attempts to take advantage of the most vulnerable: "Focus on the freshman [college] class because they will have the highest dropout rate. They often lack both the direction and funds to fully pursue their education."[42]

An unexpected obstacle for recruiters came from war veterans, especially Vietnam War veterans, who oppose the Iraq War. Jim Murphy, an administrator at West Side High in New York City, is an example of an antiwar "influencer." He organized New York Veterans Speak Out, a program in which he and other veterans speak to New York high school students. Murphy has been spreading an antiwar message since he returned from Vietnam in 1969. (On Christmas Day 1971, Murphy and a group of veterans took control of the Statue of Liberty and held it for three days, protesting the war.)

"The advantage we have in New York City," Murphy says, "is that kids tend to be a little bit cynical or skeptical about the system anyhow, so a lot of the kids just don't buy into" the Iraq War. He tries to impress those students that seem susceptible to recruiters and he gets reinforcement for the antiwar message from Iraq War returnees. "A lot of guys coming back from Iraq are not being quiet. The guys are coming back to the neighborhoods and they're not happy. They are telling their little brothers and sisters, 'No. Don't go in the service. This is not right. There's something wrong with this. You don't want to see what I saw.' We tell kids about the images you see for the rest of your life. You see the images of wanton destruction; you see bodies. Those visions don't go away." [43]

The reality of war, made public by the daily news reports of U.S. soldiers killed in Iraq, combined with growing and ever more vocal civilian opposition to the war, led the military to rethink its advertising strategy for recruits. In the fall of 2005, it budgeted a billion dollars for a five-year advertising campaign to roll out ads directed at influencers in an overt attempt to convince mothers and fathers to encourage their offspring to join the armed services.[44] Broadcast commercials urged viewers to check out www.todaysmilitary.com, where "parents/relatives" were presented with low-pressure messages about "the rewards of military service" and invited to learn about "the qualities for a successful life" in the military. Testimonies were paraded, such as one from Kelly Perdew, the winner of the reality television show *The Apprentice 2*, who attributed his success with Donald Trump to his experiences in the military. Another website launched to aid recruiters is www.goarmy.com, where the soft sell approach used at www.todaysmilitary.com is replaced with video games such as "America's Army." The teaser page promises: "You'll face your first tour of duty along with fellow soldiers. Gain experience as a Soldier in the U.S. Army without leaving home." The game, "rated 'T' for Teen," is a state-of-the-art battle simulation and a fun thrill for plenty of teenagers.

New York Congressman Charles Rangel views the Army's massive investment in advertising as an element of a more serious social rift in American society: Opportunistic politicians taking advantage of the poor. "There's no question in my mind," said Rangel, "that if we had a draft we would not be at war in Iraq, because affluent families would not want to put their kids at risk." Without a draft,

Rangel says the Army is "targeting poor white, black, and Hispanic high-schoolers in urban and rural areas with these ads."[45]

One Army commercial tries to connect manhood, education, and the military. A boy is talking to his mother about his desire to enlist in the Army and its promise of money for college. The closing line from junior to mama is a sentimental, "And besides, it's time for me to be a man." As the nationally syndicated newspaper columnist Robert Koehler points out, "What a brilliant (and shameless) manipulation of human psychology."[46] Koehler puts the Army cry for manhood into perspective by citing the work of poet Wilfred Owen, who died fighting in World War I and wrote the poem "Dulce et Decorum Est" about a comrade dying from a gas attack. The last line translates from the Latin as "It is sweet and fitting to die for one's country."

If you could hear at every jolt, the blood
Come gargling from the froth-corrupted lungs,
Obscene as cancer, bitter as the cud,
Of vile, incurable sores on innocent tongues,
My friend, you would not tell with such high
   zest
To children ardent for some desperate glory,
The old Lie: Dulce et decorum est
Pro patria mori.

7

DANIEL
The Marine Who Saw Too Much

Recruiters convinced a listless Californian named Daniel to join the Marines. On September 11, 2001, he was taking classes at a junior college near San Jose while holding down two jobs: managing a PurWater store and squeezing fruit at a Jamba Juice stand. His patriotism combined with the recruiters' sales pitches convinced him to drop out of school two units short of his associate's degree. By the next summer he was in boot camp. When we meet, the twenty-three-year-old ex-Marine asks me to restrict my identification of him to his first name; he's fighting the Veterans Administration for benefits and the Marines for an honorable discharge, and he fears publicity may hurt his case.

Daniel is slouched in his chair when we first start talking. He's wearing a camouflage baseball cap with the image of a Canada goose on its front. His black T-shirt carries the legend POW-MIA YOU ARE NOT FORGOTTEN. His forearms are covered with tattoos. His blue jeans are well faded and his black cowboy boots well worn.

"I decided my country needed me and I was pretty fit," he says about his decision to join the Marines after the attacks on the World Trade Center and the Pentagon. "I decided to go do my part. I wasn't sure what branch until I walked into the recruiting office and a Marine Corps office was before all the other ones. They kind of pulled me in, told me all their jarhead jargon, and filled my head with a whole bunch of good stuff. I was sold quickly."

Daniel speaks fast, with a slight twang and the hint of a stutter. He says his childhood stutter returned as a symptom of his combat-related post-traumatic stress disorder.

By February 2003, Daniel was trained as a radio operator and was the proud owner of a brand new Dodge Ram 1500 truck. A week after he bought the truck, he was told he was being deployed to the Middle East. "There goes my truck payments," he remembers thinking. But he parked the pickup and managed to keep the payments current while he saw the other side of the world. "It was a pretty scary time," Daniel says about his three months on a ship, patrolling Kuwaiti waters during the initial U.S. assault on Iraq.

Rotated back to the States, Daniel hopped back into the Dodge and unwound. "Came back over stateside, happy to be back. Spent all my money and had a good time. Early in 2004 we was back in the desert. This time I went directly into Iraq." He found himself on an assault boat, patrolling for "insurgents." His unit saw action in the toughest neighborhoods throughout much of 2004, often beaching the boat and joining forces with land-based troops in hot spots like Fallujah. "Pretty scary, that's all I've got to say about that," Daniel says regarding Fallujah, his speech turning percussive. "You never know when it's your time to go. Explosions from mortars going off all around you. Shots fired. You try to keep your head up. Trust the guy next to you. That's about it."

Fighting in the war flipped Daniel's political beliefs. "I came back very anti-Bush. I used to be a Republican before I joined the military. Not any more." His experiences on the ground, he says, convinced him he'd been lied to. The Iraqis "are a defeated people," he says, not a threat to America. "It's a third-world country. These people walk around with no shoes, nothing. These guys are working for a dollar a day. The military would pay the village people to come on base and build sandbags so that they can be more comfortable in their tents and pay them a dollar a day, and these guys will work making seven dollars a week just to feed their family."

Watching the construction of permanent barracks on bases in Iraq convinced Daniel that the real goal of the war was control. "Iraq is the center of the Middle East. If you control the center, you control the whole Middle East. You control all the profits that you get from there," he says about the oil reserves.

Back from leave, Daniel, who was awarded eight decorations for valor, was in for some surprises. "We go back to Camp Lejeune and we get a new CO [commanding officer] who's never been to Iraq, who doesn't have nearly as many ribbons as I do," says Daniel. "He goes, 'Get prepared to go back to Iraq in January!' This was October. We just got back. All of our jaws just dropped. He goes, 'But go home and have fun for about three weeks.'" As Daniel recounts this announcement of a third tour of duty in the Middle East in as many years, his stutter becomes much more pronounced. "I felt like a weight just got put on my chest. I couldn't breathe. Panic attacks. I can't believe this is going to happen. Everybody felt the same way. A couple of people didn't come back from leave. They decided to stay home."

Daniel looked forward to going home to California, but he realized, "I couldn't enjoy my leave because I knew I was going straight back to that hellhole I just left.

"They were trying to train us to go back," he continues. "We were well seasoned. We had to listen to these guys who had never been over there. We all thought, 'These dumb-asses are going to get us killed.' Some of these guys, they didn't know how to tie their shoes. They came back from recruiting duty wanting to get all gung ho. They were like, 'Yeah! We're going to go fight a war!' We had already been over there and seen what's happened."

This veteran of some of the worst fighting in the Iraq War, now a lance corporal and faced with a third tour of duty in the war zone, asked to see a counselor of some type, "because my head was not right." Nothing happened. He told his first sergeant that he was a conscientious objector, and he says the sergeant responded: "Get those words out of your mouth right now." Daniel was trying everything he could think of to avoid shipping out to Iraq again, and couldn't see a way out.

So he made a fateful decision.

"I was pretty frustrated," he explains. "I wanted

them to listen to me, so I decided to do something where I would stand out and get everybody's attention. I knew by doing this I would not have to go back to Iraq and harm any more people. I decided to take drugs that Friday, knowing I had a piss test on Monday. I did drugs. I did the urinalysis test on Monday. Went home for a Christmas break on Friday." Back on base after the holidays, Daniel was told he had "popped," failed the drug test.

Daniel picked cocaine as his drug of choice, convinced that if he only smoked marijuana the Marines would just slap his hand and send him packing for Iraq. He says it was the first time he had used cocaine. "I knew that if I did that they would listen to me." He finally was awarded a meeting with the battalion's commanding officer and was told that as long as he trained a replacement radio operator, he would be discharged "in a timely manner."

The day Daniel's unit shipped out to Iraq, the Marines put him on a four-day bus trip back to California, with an Other Than Honorable (OTH) discharge. "I felt really bad. I felt really bad." Other Marines in his unit failed to show up for Iraq duty, he says, and still others followed his example and used drugs in order to fail the mandatory drug test. "None of them wanted to go back, none of them did. But they did not know how to get out. I feel bad for all of them. Sometimes I wish I was with them because they were my family over there. But I have to do what I do for myself."

With three years in the Marines, two tours of duty in the war zone, eight decorations, and one bad drug test, Daniel went to the Veterans Administration in San Jose complaining of post-traumatic stress disorder, seeking help. "I showed them my papers and they said, 'Wow, you're pretty decorated. We need to get you some help.' Then they looked at the OTH and said, 'Can't do nothing for you.'" In addition to being denied help from the VA, Daniel forfeited the $1,200 the Marines took out of his first year's pay as his required contribution to qualify for GI benefits.

"I still have bad dreams every night," he says. "It's like a video that rewinds and every time I go to sleep it plays back and I wake up distraught. It just doesn't go away."

"And what are the images?" I ask him.

"War."

"What are you seeing?"

"I'm sure you've seen pictures. I don't have to describe them again. I don't want to."

But Daniel is anxious to analyze the status of affairs in Iraq from his perspective and personal experience. "A lot of innocent people get hurt over there. For the most part, their people are good. They want to raise their families. They're actually very happy that we got rid of Saddam Hussein. We had to dig a potty hole one time and we found a mass child grave. Saddam was just a bad person. These kids over there are walking around with hardly anything, barely able to feed themselves. These people are skinny. A lot of troops are giving them their extra boots. We'll give them a little bit of food. For the most part, these people just want to get on with their lives. They're not terrorists, the Iraqis. It's all the insurgents coming in from other places that misinterpret the Muslim religion. I didn't know much about Islam at the time. But I have a cross, a Catholic cross on my arm," he shows off the massive tattooed cross decorating his right arm. "A lot of them would point it out and say, 'Oh, we believe in Jesus, too. He's a prophet.' I learned a lot from the Iraqi people I got to talk to, so don't be prejudiced if you ever meet one over here. They're not bad people at all."

As for the rest of his life, "Basically I'm starting over from scratch," says Daniel. "I'm not working right now. I'm looking for a job that I'll be happy with. I'm a hard-working stiff. I've just got to find something that I'll love and enjoy. Then I'll start all over again." As for the truck? "The Dodge is gone." Repossessed.

Daniel hopes to convince the Marines to change his discharge classification so that he can be treated by the Veterans Administration for the problems he's suffering as a result of his service in Iraq. But Kit Anderton of the Resource Center for Nonviolence, the caseworker who is helping Daniel with his appeal, is not optimistic. "This is not a good path," he says about Daniel's decision to use cocaine as an exit strategy. "It is particularly not a good path if you do not have evidence that you have tried to get the attention of your commanding officer, that you've done everything you possibly can to get pastoral or psychological help. Daniel did both, but I'm not sure we're going to find evidence that he did. This was a step of desperation for him. If he had called us, we certainly would have told him not to do it." Anderton laughs with frustration. "It's really the worst thing he could have done. He's in much worse shape than he was when he enlisted."

And, I suggest, he is arguably a national hero.

"He's a national hero," Kit agrees. "When we talk about supporting the troops, what are we talking about? We're taking these kids, we're using them up and throwing them out, and not taking responsibility for it. If people knew stories like this, they wouldn't be so cavalier about saying they're supporting the troops, putting stickers on their cars, and feeling like it's done."

8

THE DEBATE AT HOME

"The whole time, they're trying to kill us," Dave Bischel tells me, speaking of his eleven-month tour of duty in Iraq. "We've been mortared. We've been shot at on a regular basis." Dave is a beefy GI who served in the Gulf War in 1991 and was called back to fight in the Iraq War. He's now a member of Iraq Veterans Against the War, and he's talking about his opposition to the war on a television talk show I'm anchoring.[47]

Dressed in a striped polo shirt and blue jeans, Dave looks relaxed as he talks about the endless stress of duty in Iraq. "The morale starts to crash and you want to blame it on somebody. You start getting angry. You start to argue amongst each other. Pretty soon you start developing this hatred almost – this hatred of Arabs. It's scary because I'm not that kind of person. I'm not that kind of person at all."

He tries to explain how he can be a good soldier and against the war at the same time. "Because I believe in serving my country doesn't mean I have to believe in the current occupation of Iraq – which I'm totally against. I understand when you enlist in the military you take on a certain responsibility to defend our interests and defend our country," he explains slowly and carefully to the nationwide television audience, quickly adding, "However, the overwhelming evidence is this is a war based on lies." Dave is challenged by viewers when I invite them to participate.

Chris calls from Mississippi to complain, "He comes on TV and knocks our military down and knocks our soldiers down."

Dave is specific with his reply. "This is an unjust, immoral war based on lies," he explains. "Our soldiers are being killed and wounded for nothing."

Chris is not satisfied. "It just seems to me any time the government needs to make a decision, we have naysayers out there who will second-guess them. We don't need our military coming out and downgrading our military."

Dave listens, and politely repeats that it is his support of his fellow troops that fuels his work against the war.

Mary calls next, from Pennsylvania. "That gentleman sitting on the TV has me very, very upset." Her voice is shaking with emotion as she continues. "My son was injured in Iraq, and as far as I'm concerned, people like him who come back from Iraq and knock our soldiers and say they are so low, they are so depressed, are full of crap."

Dave makes it clear again he is not knocking soldiers. "That's exactly what you're doing." It's impossible not to feel sympathy for Mary as she continues. "My son has come back. He has been hurt. You're saying our president has done something wrong." Her voice starts to crack as she rationalizes the war by citing Saddam Hussein's abuses of Iraqis.

"Mary," Dave says softly. "Mary, you do understand that our country, during the Reagan era, sold weapons of mass destruction to Saddam Hussein. You do understand that? Why wasn't it a concern then, Mary?"

"Because we didn't have a president," she spits out, "with the guts to stand up and say, 'Enough is enough.'"

By the end of the summer in 2005, polls showed public exasperation with the Bush administration war policies. A September Gallup poll showed 67 percent of Americans disapproving of the way Bush was handling the war, and 59 percent agreeing that the United States had "made a mistake" by sending troops there. And, in a tragic commentary on the war and its results, when asked, "All in all, do you think it was worth going to war in Iraq, or not?" 53 percent of Americans answered with a resounding, "Not worth it."

As the mood of the nation moved against the Iraq War, it appeared that even *Beetle Bailey* joined the loyal opposition. In a single panel, the comic strip's creators, Mort and Greg Walker, showed Beetle's platoon in a room. One is dressed as a clown; another holds up a sign that reads LET'S TALK; Beetle sits behind a desk marked JOKES; another desk is marked FREE SWEETS; behind it a drawing of a dove is on the wall; still another soldier is dressed up as Santa Claus. "What's this?" asks the general. He's told, "We're studying alternatives to warfare."[48]

Meanwhile, throughout the war the U.S. military

has refused to estimate how many Iraqis – military and civilian – its forces have killed. "The Defense Department doesn't maintain a comprehensive or authoritative count of Iraqi casualties," Pentagon spokesman Greg Hicks reiterated to reporters when he released a report that did estimate the number of Iraqi civilians killed and injured by "insurgents."[49] In November 2005, the independent organization Iraq Body Count estimated that as many as 30,000 Iraqi civilians had been killed by military forces since the U.S. invasion.[50] A year earlier, a study in the peer-reviewed British medical journal *The Lancet* estimated that 100,000 Iraqi civilians – more than half of them women and children – died as a direct result of the war just in its first year.[51]

Just before she was killed in Iraq, humanitarian aid worker Marla Ruzicka wrote a report from Baghdad suggesting that the military did indeed keep an accounting; it simply was not releasing the figures. "A good place to search for Iraqi civilian death counts," Ruzicka wrote, "is the Iraqi Assistance Center in Baghdad and the General Information Centers set up by the U.S. military across Iraq. Iraqis who have been harmed by Americans have the right to file claims for compensation at these locations, and some claims have been paid." She cited the records kept of such payments as an obvious database for the civilian costs of the war. "These statistics demonstrate," she pointed out, "that the U.S. military can and does track civilian casualties."[52]

As to the war's cost in cash, the Nobel

Prize–winning Columbia University economist Joseph Stiglitz estimated it at $2 trillion early in 2006. That number quadruples congressional estimates (and congressional estimates dwarf White House estimates) because Stiglitz factors in long-term medical costs for veterans, the increased price of oil, the overall impact of the war on the U.S. economy, and other ongoing negative effects that others overlooked. "I think two trillion dollars is conservative," said Stiglitz when he presented his findings.

To make matters worse, the military further alienated the parents of some fallen soldiers with a postmortem propaganda play: inscribing OPERATION IRAQI FREEDOM on the tombstones of Iraq War veterans buried at Arlington National Cemetery. The Pentagon initiated its policy of naming its military operations with the 1989 invasion of Panama, which was tagged "Operation Just Cause." The idea of branding wars was an attempt to frame the nature of and increase public support for U.S. military operations. Most military gravestones at Arlington are inscribed with basic information – name, rank, and dates of birth and death. If the soldier fought in a war, that is noted.

Not all families chose the option of adding OPERATION IRAQI FREEDOM to the tombstones of their relatives, but some found the grave markers so inscribed without their approval. "I was a little taken aback," was the response of Robert McCaffrey upon seeing the Iraq War brand on the gravestone supplied to the family by the government. His son Patrick was killed in Iraq in 2004. The deeply grieving father's words were measured when he was asked about the inscription: "In one way, I feel it's taking advantage to a small degree." But he expressed no doubt about his son's role in the war. "Patrick did not want to be there, that is a definite fact."[53]

On November 30, 2005, President Bush used the last words of a soldier killed in Iraq to sell his ongoing war. "Before our mission in Iraq is accomplished," Bush lectured midshipmen at the Naval Academy in Annapolis, "there will be tough days ahead. A time of war is a time of sacrifice, and we've lost some very fine men and women in this war on terror." The President identified as an example Marine Corporal Jeff Starr, "who was killed fighting the terrorists in Ramadi earlier this year. After he died," Bush reported, "a letter was found on his laptop computer. Here's what he wrote. He said, 'If you're reading this, then I've died in Iraq. I don't regret going. Everybody dies, but few get to do it for something as important as freedom. It may seem confusing why we are in Iraq, it's not to me. I'm here helping these people, so they can live the way we live. Not to have to worry about tyrants or vicious dictators. Others have died for my freedom, now this is my mark.'

"There is only one way to honor the sacrifice of Corporal Starr and his fallen comrades," insisted the President, "and that is to take up their mantle, carry on their fight, and complete their mission." That argument had begun facing stiff opposition, more and more of it from within the ranks of Bush's own party.

As the U.S. body count rose in 2005 and Iraq slipped toward civil war, even some Republicans in Congress stopped merely questioning the war and began actively calling for its end. "We're locked into a bogged-down problem, not dissimilar to where we were in Vietnam. The longer we stay, the more problems we're going to have," decided Senator Chuck Hagel (R-Neb.). "We should start figuring out how we get out of there. Stay the course is not a policy. I think by any standard, when you analyze two and a half years in Iraq where we have put in over a third of a trillion dollars, where we have lost almost 1,900 Americans, over 14,000 wounded, electricity production down, oil production down – any measurement, any standard you apply to this, we're not winning." [54]

Five weeks later, Vietnam veteran and Reagan administration National Security Agency director Lieutenant General William Odom called the Iraq War "the greatest strategic disaster in United States history, far worse than Vietnam." [55]

Historian and World War II veteran Howard Zinn, after a lifetime studying and making history, both as a university professor and as a peace activist, rejected the excuses for the Iraq War when we talked shortly after the invasion. "It's good Saddam Hussein is gone, but at what expense? Ten to fifteen thousand Iraqis dead – no one knows the exact count. Many more injured, mutilated – no one knows exactly. And Iraq is no closer to democracy. It is in chaos, and violence continues every day. It is a brutal occupation. It corroborates something I believe is true about war, even wars that seem to accomplish something good: The means of war are horrible, the ends uncertain."[56]

Marine Corps Major Paul Hackett came back from serving in Iraq vehemently opposed to the war, but he favored a continued U.S. troop presence there until an Iraqi army became adequately trained to secure the country. In a special election for Congress in 2005 – the first such run by an Iraq War veteran – he came close to beating his Republican opponent in an Ohio district that had voted overwhelmingly for President Bush. During the campaign, Hackett publicly called his commander-in-chief a "chicken hawk" for not fighting in Vietnam, and he condemned Bush as the biggest threat facing the United States.[57] Hackett did not back away from the verbal assaults even when given a chance. "I said it, I mean it, I stand by it," he reiterated well after the election. "Bush is a chicken hawk, okay? Tough shit."[58]

Hackett first joined the Marines in 1982, while he was a university student. Before he reenlisted, he'd already put in sixteen years, three of them on active duty. In his campaign literature, Hackett announced that he opposed the war prior to reenlisting in the Marines. "I was against the war," he wrote. "It was a misuse of our military that damaged our credibility throughout the world and squandered our political capital. Still, I volunteered to serve, and I have no regrets."[59]

Just before Thanksgiving Day 2005, Congressman John Murtha, a Democrat from Pennsylvania with a thirty-seven-year Marine Corps career, a highly decorated Vietnam War combat veteran who is respected by both Republicans and Democrats for his expertise on military affairs and who had voted for the invasion of Iraq, finally said enough is enough. Racked with emotion, Murtha insisted that further fighting in Iraq would be a lost cause. He called for the United States "to immediately redeploy U.S. troops consistent with the safety of U.S. forces." Just back from visiting American troops in Iraq, Murtha reported that the war was ruining the U.S. military.

"The future of our military is at risk," said Murtha. "Our military and their families are stretched thin. Many say that the Army is broken. Some of our troops are on their third deployment. Recruitment is down, even as our military has lowered its standards. Defense budgets are being cut. Personnel costs are skyrocketing, particularly in health care. Choices will have to be made. We cannot allow promises we have made to our military families in terms of service benefits, in terms of their health care, to be negotiated away. Procurement programs that ensure our military dominance cannot be negotiated away. We must be prepared. The war in Iraq has caused huge shortfalls at our bases in the U.S. Much of our ground equipment is worn out and in need of either serious overhaul or replacement. George Washington said, 'To be prepared for war is one of the most effective means of preserving peace.' We must rebuild our Army." [60]

After Murtha's about-face, Vice President Dick Cheney complained, with obvious reference to Murtha, "Some of the most irresponsible comments have, of course, come from politicians who actually voted in favor of authorizing force against Saddam Hussein." Cheney was speaking to a friendly audience at the conservative Frontiers of Freedom Institute as he brazened on, "The President and I cannot prevent certain politicians from losing their memory, or their backbone – but we're not going to sit by and let them rewrite history." [61]

Murtha lashed back, "I like guys who've never been there that criticize us who've been there." His voice rose with disgust. "I like that," he said again, and then targeted the Vice President. "I like guys who got five deferments and never been there and send people to war and then don't like to hear suggestions about what needs to be done." He was pounding the table with anger.[62]

Many other critics were quick to point out the military records – or lack thereof – of the key figures in the Bush administration: President Bush missed the Vietnam War by signing up for sporadic National Guard service; Karl Rove, Bush's senior advisor, also managed to skip Vietnam; Vice President Cheney famously said he had "other priorities" during the war and sought serial student deferments; Cheney's chief of staff, Lewis "Scooter" Libby, a prime architect of the Iraq War, avoided Vietnam while studying at Yale; Defense Secretary Donald Rumsfeld studied at Princeton instead of fighting in Korea; former Deputy Defense Secretary Paul Wolfowitz, an early and furious Iraq War proponent, also managed to dodge military service in Vietnam.

★★★

In the middle of the scorching summer of 2005, the Veterans for Peace organization staged its annual meeting at the University of Dallas campus at Irving, a liberal arts school built in the 1960s as a bastion of Catholic conservatism. Despite the muggy heat, the group's director says that location was chosen because it "is the heart of Bush country," a short drive from the president's ranch in Crawford.

In the university's parking lot sits a big old school bus, repainted a brilliant red, white, and blue and spangled with stars. Across the back of the bus is painted this verse from the Cuban poet Jose Marti:

> *I cultivate a white rose*
> *In July as in January*
> *For the sincere friend*
> *Who gives me his hand frankly.*
> *And for the cruel person who tears out*
> *The heart with which I live,*
> *Cultivate neither nettles nor thorns;*
> *I cultivate a white rose.*

The vast majority of those gathered for the conference are grizzled Vietnam War veterans, identified not only by patches that call out VIETNAM VETERANS AGAINST THE WAR, but also by their salt-and-pepper beards and their graying, balding heads. One is dressed up in an Uncle Sam suit, holding high a placard that reads, "I am addicted to war. Please help me."

Sitting around one table inside is a handful of Iraq War veterans, now against the war. For well over an hour the men trade war stories – horrified by their memories. One of them is Michael Hoffman, a founder of Iraq Veterans Against the War, which at the time boasted a membership of 200. Hoffman explains, "We're trying to educate people based on what we've learned from all this pain and suffering." And they've learned plenty.

"We were shooting artillery in built-up areas," another of the group, Abdul Henderson, offers. "You just see people running. Cars flying down the street. People falling off bikes. This is sad. You sit there and you look in your binos [binoculars] and you see these artillery shells blowing these buildings up and you see people just crying. It's just – damn – you feel sorry. These people don't have drinking water. They have no electricity. They're living in very third-world conditions. Here we are just bombing the city with artillery. All this shrapnel just tearing people to shreds." His voice is exasperated. "I felt sorry for those people."

"Most of what you've heard us describe," says Charlie Anderson as the stories of wanton killing and destruction continue, "constitute war crimes. Not on our part, but on the part of our government. Because they knew that all of the reasons they sent us there were lies. We weren't going there for weapons of mass destruction, terrorists, or to plant freedom. We were going there for imperialism and they were manufacturing consent. It was not that we were doing this great noble thing. I realized that when I came back. My easy answer for why I didn't go again is PTSD. But the deeper moral side is that I was not going to be involved in the perpetration of a crime against humanity."

The Iraq veterans are asked if they have a message for President Bush. Abdul jumps at the opportunity to express his disgust. "I see this guy in the most prestigious office in the history of the world, and this guy takes it for a joke. A guy who says, 'Bring it on.' A guy who ain't never been shot at, a guy who ain't never seen another man die, a guy who ain't never seen people live in utter fear for their existence, saying, 'Bring it on,' in the safety and security of twenty-four-hour protection from the government at our expense. He gets to act like a cowboy from a Western movie. It's totally sickening to me."

"I would look him straight in the eye and ask him, 'Why?'" says Michael Hoffman. "And I would hold him there and make him answer me. He never has to deal with us one-on-one." His voice rises with disgust and frustration. "I dare him to talk to any of us like that – one-on-one – and give us an answer."

Veterans for Peace urged members of Congress to initiate impeachment proceedings against both President Bush and Vice President Cheney, citing "a war of aggression on Iraq" and "a growing and appalling series of what must legally be considered war crimes and crimes against humanity in the execution of that war." [63]

That same summer, President Bush and his handlers offered up their latest rationalization for continuing the war: We must keep fighting because U.S. soldiers had been killed. In what was billed by the Bush administration as a major policy address on the war, the president called it "vital to the future security of our country." He acknowledged the war's brutality, but defended it as necessary. "Like most Americans, I see the images of violence and bloodshed. Every picture is horrifying, and the suffering is real. Amid all this violence, I know Americans ask the question: Is the sacrifice worth it?" He immediately answered his own question, "It is worth it."

The speech was given to an audience of soldiers, a sea of red berets, gathered at the headquarters of the 82nd Airborne Division and Army's Special Operations unit at Fort Bragg, North Carolina. "To the soldiers in this hall, and our servicemen and women across the globe: I thank you for your courage under fire and your service to our nation," Bush said. "I thank our military families – the burden of war falls especially hard on you. In this war, we have lost good men and women who left our shores to defend freedom and did not live to make the journey home. I've met with families grieving the loss of loved ones who were taken from us too soon. I've been inspired by their strength in the face of such great loss. We pray for the families. And the best way to honor the lives that have been given in this struggle is to complete the mission." [64]

Garrett Reppenhagen was a sniper in Iraq through most of 2004. He says he joined the military, just before the attacks on the Pentagon and the Twin Towers, "for a lot of reasons. I was a high school dropout. I was on my own, pretty much finding myself at a dead end." Working three jobs but still unable to meet car and house payments, Garrett filed for bankruptcy – and enlisted. "I made an extreme decision. My dad was a soldier. He was in Vietnam. I thought, If he could've done it, I can do it too. I joined up." He joined with a buddy, Jeff Englehardt, who is also now opposed to the war. "I basically joined," allows Jeff, "because I was just bored. I took a year of college and I dropped out. A lot of it had to do with jumping into the great unknown and seeing the world of authority and structure, and seeing how I would manage with that. And I really wanted to see Germany and I really wanted to get the college money. At the time it was a great idea."

Garrett was at the Dallas airport, heading home for a two-week leave, when he had second thoughts about having joined the Army. At the time, U.S. forces were crossing the Kuwait-Iraq border, heading toward Baghdad. "In the airport, every TV was showing it over and over again: Bush giving his ultimatum," he recalls. "It came down to the last hour. It was showing the air strikes on the TV and the tanks crossing the line into the desert. The cities were just blowing up. I remember the entire airport was cheering. I just stood there – I was in uniform – completely just alienated from everybody I was looking at. I kind of made up my mind then that something was completely wrong."

The invasion simply reinforced feelings Jeff and Garrett had been developing since basic training.

Neither believed the official reasons for the Iraq invasion, and they expected that they would be able to avoid the combat theater because they had just served nine months as peacekeepers in Kosovo. No such luck.

Nonetheless, Garrett chose to be a sniper in Iraq. "Part of me thought I could actually make a difference. I thought that maybe me behind the trigger is better than Joe Snuffy behind the trigger, just shooting at anybody with a stick. I decided I'd rather have me behind the trigger because I could make a better moral decision about who I'm going to kill."

When they got to Iraq, they started a blog with the mission statement: "This site is the mouthpiece for a group of soldiers who are fighting in a war they oppose for a President they didn't elect while the petrochemical complex turns the blood of their fallen comrades into oil." [65]

"We wrote about what we saw," Jeff says. "A lot of it was emotional. A lot of it was very raw. We don't regret it one bit." When their commanders discovered the blog, he says the Army considered a court-martial against them because of the antiwar messages they were circulating. "It was very stressful, because it felt like there was an enemy on both sides of the wire." There was no court-martial, but he remembers with disgust, "We did get chastised for being 'commie antiwar peace-freak faggots.'"

In a final posting on the blog, after returning to the U.S. with an honorable discharge, Jeff reflected on his civilian life. "Everyday I see myself in the mirror and am reminded of the new person who stares back. A new me, a refined me. A happy and optimistic me. A fresh mold, a new start. Things will be better now, for I am free and very gratefully alive. The future seems so bright and pure now compared to where I was only a few short months ago. I am in control of my own life again."

It is a far different message and tone than what Jeff and his blog partners had been posting while in Iraq. "I joined for the wrong reasons," Jeff wrote from Baquba. "I had no idea I could go to war, kill without a thought and serve the purposes of self-righteous neocons, but here I am, and this whole world crisis is mere evidence of what can go wrong when a whole nation in apathy allows ignorance and greed to turn the gears in the combine.

"Now I am at war with freedom fighters who want their simple way of life back from gun-toting rednex and war mongers, regardless of who is in charge, because although they will always be oppressed and poor, at least they will be alive. I want to help right the wrong, but for now can only fight for my life.

"I have killed, but where is the remorse? Better his mom crying than mine. If you think any different about pulling the trigger you're as good as dead. Live to fight another day. I will atone for these crimes on a day when I am not shackled to the rules that bind my mouth from a subversive tongue and force my free will to hide amongst the shadows.

"Do not be deceived by the greed mongers and war hawks who run our great country. Seek truth and strive for reform. The best way to counter terrorism is to not participate in it. War is not the solution, and until we realize this, no one is safe."

At the 2005 Veterans for Peace conference near Dallas, Jeff and Garrett had only been out of the Army for a couple of months. Both were continuing their antiwar work as activist members of Iraq Veterans Against the War, convinced, as Garrett says, that as other Iraq War veterans are mustered out of the armed services, the nascent movement of antiwar veterans will grow. "It's going to take some time for these soldiers to come back, realize they've been fucked, and get their shit together. They're going to get pissed off, and they're going to be looking for groups like Veterans for Peace and Iraq Veterans Against the War to join so they can finally get some feeling of completion and of a good feeling that, 'I've been a soldier for the last four years of my life, hurting people. Now I want to help, I want to do some good.'"

As part of his antiwar work, Jeff Englehardt wants those considering a military career to know the realities of the Iraq War. "Imagine yourself looking down the sights of an M14 rifle and pulling the trigger on a man that just wants to help liberate his country," he says, speaking rapid-fire and with the passion that comes from experience and despair. "How would you feel? To kill someone, that's one thing. But to actually witness on an almost weekly basis an Iraqi that gets victimized by a car bomb, to see the carnage, to see the blood and the guts laying on the side of the road, to see a little girl's pink sandal smoldering, with her foot still in it, smoldering in the gutter, these are images that you're going to have to live with the rest of your life. I'm dealing with it. Just think about that when you sign that paper, that contract to dedicate yourself to being a mercenary killer for the Bush administration and his corporate buddies."

Leading up to the March 2003 invasion of Iraq, antiwar protests were breaking out all over the world, and Kelly Dougherty was sure war was not the answer. Yet she found herself utterly compromised. "I definitely would have been at the protests had I not been at the Army base training for war," she says with a laugh that comes easily, especially when it accents what she sees as the absurdity of the Iraq War. "It was a big conflict for me. I thought a lot of times, 'Oh, I should resist. I should refuse to go. I should take a public stance.'" She laments the fact that many of those in the military who have taken a vocal and public position against the war are told that they are cowards. "I would say it takes a lot more courage to refuse to go and to stand up against the status quo and all your fellow soldiers than it takes to just go along with it."

But go along with it she did. Kelly had been in the National Guard for seven years when her unit was shipped to the Middle East. Once there, the well-spoken former University of Colorado student found compatriots just as reticent about the assignment as she was. "My friends and I would discuss refusing. We would discuss the point at which we were going to refuse to follow orders because we felt that they were putting our lives in complete danger. But as much as we talked, we never did anything. When it came right down to it, you're either going to have to take a stand and suffer all these consequences or you're going to have to suffer maybe the ultimate consequence, which is death. It was like, death is uncertain. I know that if I refuse I'm going to get court-martialed. So I guess I'll just choose possible death."

Kelly was against the occupation when she arrived in Iraq, and what she learned while on duty there only reinforced her opinion. "We got over there and no weapons of mass destruction, no terrorism except that which we created," she says. "What were we doing? We were protecting ourselves. We were sent halfway around the world so we can protect ourselves. We could have protected ourselves much easier back in Colorado." She says others in her unit – who initially were gung ho about the war – began to question their roles.

At one point during her Iraq tour, Kelly's father was relatively nearby. He came to Baghdad as a peace activist, demonstrating against the war with the full support of his military police officer daughter.

Kelly was an MP with the 220th Military Police Company, stationed in the desert of southern Iraq, often sent out to guard broken-down Halliburton fuel tankers. The U.S. commanders feared these "assets" were vulnerable to desperate Iraqis frustrated by the long post-invasion lines at their civilian gas stations. Usually, after hours of such guard duty, Kelly and her colleagues would be informed that there were no spare tank trucks available to transfer the precious fuel from the disabled tanker they were busy guarding. "We'd wait there two hours, three hours, four hours, and get the call, 'Oh, we're sorry. We can't send a recovery vehicle.' So we always knew, when we went to guard a vehicle, when we shot people with nonlethal ammunition, when we maced people, when we hit them, when we yelled at them, when we got into physical confrontations – we knew that we would just be abandoning the vehicle to them or we would be burning it. We would burn an asset. Not only is fuel valuable to the Americans, but fuel is even more valuable to the Iraqis." It was as incomprehensible to the MPs as it was to the Iraqis. "They would just look at us like, 'What are you doing in our country? You're bringing in something that we don't have and you're destroying it in front of our faces.' It was so frustrating."

We're talking on the grounds of the University of Dallas, where Kelly had come for the Veterans for Peace conference, and the chiming bells in the tower punctuate the music of a guitarist sitting on the lawn, strumming and singing. It is the 1965 Phil Ochs anthem "I Ain't Marching Anymore." The ballad recites a litany of American wars, with the still-timely refrain:

> It's always the old to lead us to the war
> It's always the young to fall
> Now look at all we've won with the sabre and
>   the gun
> Tell me is it worth it all?

It wasn't worth it all for Kelly. She served out her tour of duty in Iraq because she was worried about the consequences of refusing orders, and she felt an obligation to stay with her unit, which included an old high-school friend. "We shouldn't have gone over there in the first place," she says of the U.S. invasion. "Our presence there was aggravating everything. It was creating hostility between Iraqis which hadn't necessarily been there before. It was creating poverty. It was creating desperation. It was creating violence and death. We were there as a foreign occupying army telling people what to do, going in there acting like we owned the country – because basically we do. It's run by the United States." Quitting Iraq would be the most positive next step for both America and Iraq, she says. "They only started civilization between the Tigris and Euphrates Rivers, but they're not smart enough to figure it out now," she says sarcastically, her tone etched by disgust.

Kelly came home, received an honorable discharge in August 2004, and helped found Iraq Veterans Against the War. She is motivated to speak out against the war by experiences such as the one she had retrieving film from a shopkeeper once she returned home. "The photo-shop lady almost started crying because she was so moved that I had served in Iraq. I just thought, 'If you only knew what we were doing over there. We're not building schools and repairing waterlines. We're burning fuel trucks and hitting people with sticks and shooting them with rubber bullets. For no reason. Raiding their houses.

Creating catastrophe. If you only knew!' You just want to shake people." Her usually calm voice tenses with frustration. "But they're really speaking from their hearts. They don't know. They do really care about what they think you're doing. You just want to shake them and snap them out of it."

9

ROBERT ZABALA
The Marine Outsider

Robert Zabala's grandfather was awarded a Purple Heart for being wounded in combat during his service in Vietnam; his mother and father were in the Navy, as were all his uncles; and a cousin was a Marine. Looking for some structure and feeling a sense of duty to his country, Robert decided to sign up for the Marine Corps reserves when he was accepted at the University of California, Santa Cruz.

He graduated from boot camp after the U.S. invasion of Iraq, but as he got to know his fellow Marines during training, he says he began to feel estranged. "Everybody resigned themselves to killing somebody. I started to question – maybe that's not right."

We are talking on a typically sunny Santa Cruz day in a downtown park. Robert sits straight-backed at a picnic table. His hair is brush-cut, accenting his steel-rimmed glasses. He is soft-spoken but direct, often referring to notes to check dates as he tells his story.

Robert says he first was caught off guard during physical training. "They teach you how to punch. The instructor says, 'Punch!' The recruits' response is, 'Kill!'" This is typical Marine training. Marines are carefully trained and highly disciplined warriors meant to be used against an enemy the government wants dead.

Robert was bothered that the word "kill" was perpetually used to motivate the recruits. "Kill" was the mandated response when recruits were ordered to the ground for push-ups. "They say, 'Starting positions!' And everybody just drops and they say, 'Kill!' Everything they do is 'Kill!' and I seemed to be the only one who wasn't screaming as loud or saying it with zeal or passion. It just didn't feel right."

Another turning point for Robert was the announcement that the U.S. military had killed Saddam Hussein's sons in Baghdad. (During Saddam's rule, his sons were widely feared as impulsive brutes and murderers.) "The drill instructors started cheering and the recruits got all excited and I started thinking: Should I really be cheering for someone who just died?"

Then came the sad day when a recruit turned a rifle on himself and committed suicide on the rifle range. Robert was part of an assembly called by a captain charged with reporting the news to recruits. He looks down at his notes, careful to make sure he quotes the captain correctly. "He said, 'Fuck him. Fuck his parents for raising him and fuck the girl who dumped him.' He went on, attacking this kid's character, insulting his parents for even having sex and bringing this child into this world. It was a total disregard for the sanctity of human life."

Robert says he looked at the faces of the men in his platoon as the captain ranted and raved. They were emotionless, a fact that he found as disturbing as the captain's speech. It was the same captain who had shown a motivational video portraying firefights to the platoon during training, complete with tanks firing, the tracks of tracer rounds, and multiple images of dead bodies on the battlefield. The soundtrack was the Eminem song "Let the Bodies Hit the Floor." The refrain "Let the bodies hit the floor" is repeatedly chanted to heavy metal guitar riffs and is periodically interrupted by verses like this:

Skin against skin, blood and bone
You're all by yourself, but you're not alone
You wanted in, now you're here
Driven by hate, consumed by fear.

As the video played, Robert says he looked around at his fellow Marines and watched them nod their heads, tapping their feet to the beat, smiling. "I was feeling kind of disgusted. Why were we watching this? They were getting off on this. They were really getting excited and pumped up."

Although he felt like he didn't belong, Robert marked the time, intent on completing boot camp. He passed at the top of his class, started school, and joined his Marine unit, which had just returned from fighting in Iraq. He introduced himself to the other guys, and they introduced him to one of their post-Iraq pastimes – trading war-zone snapshots of Iraqis they'd killed, covered with blood. "It seemed as if they were trading baseball cards. It was disgusting."

His first year out of boot camp, Robert – back at the university – switched majors from computer engineering to literature, switched his religious affiliation from Catholicism to Buddhism, and started seriously questioning his emotional and philosophical fitness for the Marine Corps. That's when he decided to call the GI Rights Hotline.

Robert wants out of the Marine Corps. In mid-2003, he filed an application to be recognized as a conscientious objector, and he's brought his carefully written claim to our meeting. Point by point it argues his case: how he went from "Gung ho!" to "I won't go."

Robert read the definition of a conscientious objector and thought he was reading a description of himself. "You ever heard that song 'Piña Colada'? The singer is reading off that description and he realizes, 'Hey, this is my wife!' I was reading the CO description and I realized – hey, this is me! I wanted my conscientious objector discharge. If they put me in a nonfighting job, I still saw myself as a cog in the Marine Corps machine."

Robert pushes his folder across the table to me and I read through his CO application, beginning with his nonnegotiable declaration, "I will no longer participate in an organization that sustains war." And to make sure there is no misunderstanding, he further writes, "I refuse to aid in any way anything that would violently rip someone's life from this world. I shall not be the one to cause the suffering that the loss of one life brings. I cannot take part in an organization that prepares to kill human life. I will not take part in killing. I will not aid in killing."

(Robert's statement reminded me of my own CO

application, filed during the Vietnam War in 1968. "I am conscientiously opposed to all war and killing," I wrote. "My religious training," I explained, "taught me to believe that God is life, and that participation in war in any form is anti life." My CO application was denied, but the Army eventually chose not to draft me after a Selective Service psychiatrist advised against it, calling me "a markedly eccentric young man, completely incapable of fitting into or complying with any authority structure.")

Robert's CO application refers explicitly to his negative boot-camp experiences. He writes about the captain that denigrated the recruit who committed suicide on the rifle range, "He worked [recruits] into a frenzy with his speeches about 'blowing shit up' and 'kicking some fucking ass.' I didn't understand how someone could be so motivated to kill." He recounts watching Iraq War veterans trade photographs of war victims. "I wonder what the families of the dead people would feel if they knew that their son, brother, or niece was photographed for sport."

Finally, Robert indicts the mission of the Marines. "I began to think about the thousands of people who died in the past year in war, who didn't die due to just one soldier or suicide bomber, but largely by an organization," he writes. "This organization trains to kill human life. This organization also places mission accomplishment above human life. Every part of the Marine Corps, be it Radio Operator to Food Preparation, participates to keep this organization moving along on its mission to end human life."

Robert is confident he will be mustered out of the Corps as a CO: "I will get my conscientious objector discharge. I will make the Marine Corps see me as a conscientious objector regardless of what anybody says. If they reject my claim I'm going to appeal. I want to do this the right way. I don't want to just go AWOL. I want them to know there are conscientious objectors." And he hopes to influence others. "I want them to know that Marines have come up to me asking me how to be a conscientious objector." The Pentagon says 110 service members filed conscientious objector applications in 2004, four times the number in 2000, according to a February 8, 2006, report in the *Wall Street Journal*.

While his paperwork migrates through the system, Robert shows up at his unit for reserve duty, but with a long list of stipulations. After filing for CO status, Robert drew his own line in the sand. "I said, 'Sergeant, I won't do this, this and this. I won't touch ammunition. I won't touch weapons. I won't take apart weapons. If someone has to go to the bathroom and asks me to hold a rifle, I won't do it, et cetera, et cetera, et cetera.' He said, 'Okay. I respect that.'" The next time Robert was assigned to hand out ammunition to his fellow Marines, he says, "I just sat there reading *The Iliad*."

10

A CULTURE OF PEACE

April Burns, whose husband was killed in Vietnam, was on duty when 21-year-old Marine Lance Corporal Robert Zabala picked up his phone and punched in the GI Rights Hotline number. The hotline is a network of nonprofit, nongovernmental counseling agencies that provides no-questions-asked help and information to members of the military about discharges, grievance and complaint procedures, and other civil rights.

Among the hotline's member groups is the Resource Center for Nonviolence, founded in 1967 by Vietnam War resisters. It is headquartered in an old Santa Cruz beach house. Books are for sale in the meeting room – separated into categories with names like "War and Its Causes" and "Conscientious Objector Info" – as are bumper stickers with the familiar legends MAKE LOVE NOT WAR and PEACE IS PATRIOTIC, the latter sporting doves in place of stars in a stylized rendition of Old Glory. Photographs showing the crowds at peace marches worldwide before the start of the Iraq War line a section of wall. Here the GI Rights Hotline committee gets together weekly to hash out strategy, work through game plans for specific cases, and – periodically – share tales of successes. The day I join them, April Burns leads the meeting, which she starts with a moment of silence.

Later, Burns and I meet at the little White Raven coffee house in Fenton, a crossroads a few miles up into the Santa Cruz Mountains from the city of Santa Cruz. The White Raven is a relaxed hangout with friendly conversation and upbeat music, where the counter help are characters who announce orders with calls like, "Here's a latte that looks so good I'm about to take a few sips!" The comfortable atmosphere reflects a carefree life, far from our sobering talk of war and Vietnam and Iraq.

Burns tells me her first husband was drafted by the Marines and killed in Vietnam in 1967. She was working at Oak Knoll Naval Hospital in Oakland at the time, and the facility was filled with wounded from the Vietnam War. "I got to see what the war was about first-hand in a really clear, uncensored way," she says. "That affected me tremendously."

She's wearing a white peasant blouse with blue jeans and gold hoop earrings. Her grandson is with us at the table, talking about a promised trip to a skateboard park later that morning, sipping his soy milk hot chocolate. Since those Vietnam War days, she's been active in what she calls "peace work" and "cultural engineering." The 1991 Gulf War motivated her to join forces with the Resource Center for Nonviolence. She met and worked with members of the military who opposed American military intervention then, and many of those veterans actively support and counsel resisters to the Iraq War.

The case studies pour out of her. Burns tells the story of a soldier who called the hotline for help, a young man from the Midwest who refused to go back to the war zone. "He told me, 'When I was on a tank and the children would come up around the tank, we would throw them food. One time I saw a child and she looked like she was my daughter. I couldn't distinguish anymore between that child and my child.' He said, 'When I came home and I saw my daughter again, I knew I couldn't be part of it. I couldn't go back. I couldn't do it. I wouldn't do it.'"

Burns and her colleagues help soldiers prepare their petitions for discharge as conscientious objectors. Military rules mandate that in order for a soldier to qualify as a CO, an epiphany must occur *after* the soldier is in the military. The claim must be based on moral, ethical, or religious grounds, but it must involve a personal experience of change. It's tough to convince the military's investigating officers to rule in favor of the petitioner.

"I believe there is a culture of war and a culture of peace," says Burns. "We must keep the culture of peace vital and alive. That requires generations and it requires consistency and it requires commitment. But it's a strong culture." She tells the resisters she counsels that they have what she calls the resistance strain of humanity. "There's a long river that they're part of. And they need to know that, and we're a part of that with them. I want to be in that river. That's who I am. I'm not naïve enough at this point in my life to ever believe that this struggle will no longer exist. But there has to be this critical mass of people who are conscious and acting with their hands and feet.

"They feel so alone," she says of resisters to the war. "They feel so strange. They feel out of step. Robert Zabala talks about that."

Just off Broadway in downtown Oakland, California, there's a clutch of old office buildings where it looks as if time stopped in the forties. Air conditioners hang out of the wood-framed windows. The storefront shops are filled with newsagents, luncheonettes, and barbers. At Fourteenth and Franklin, the Financial Center Building sports fierce-looking eagles in bas-relief profile on its elegant façade. A frosted-glass art deco lamp hangs in the two-story entryway. Only the sign in the coffee shop offering espresso keeps the corner from looking as if World War II just ended. Upstairs, on the second floor, a small suite of offices is jammed with a mishmash of desks covered with file folders and papers, binders and books. The walls are papered with posters: STUCK BETWEEN IRAQ AND A HARD PLACE, and CUT AND RUN IN AN IMMORAL WAR – IT'S THE MORAL THING TO DO, and that old standby from the Vietnam War, complete with the familiar flower, WAR IS NOT HEALTHY FOR CHILDREN AND OTHER LIVING THINGS. This is the West Coast office of the Central Committee for Conscientious Objectors, just across Broadway from the Oakland Army Induction Center where, a generation and a divisive war ago, I was ordered by my draft board to appear for induction into the U.S. Army.

This is one of the boiler rooms where the telephone

rings (and is immediately answered) when a scared, frustrated, abused, or sick soldier calls the GI Rights Hotline. The hotline's posters, calling out to active duty, National Guard, and reserve troops and offering to help them, can be spotted near military bases at coffeehouses, bars, and bookstores – wherever GIs are sure to congregate. And organizers say the hotline phone number and website address is carved on military base bunks by soldiers trying to help their brothers and sisters in arms.

The day I visit, Louise Zimmerman is on duty. With gray hair and glasses, the former schoolteacher now volunteers to sit by the phone waiting for frightened and worried calls from soldiers and their families.

Zimmerman taught English, and English as a second language, in Concord and east San Jose before she retired. Experiences in the classroom led her to volunteer for the hotline. She watched as the military recruited her non-English speaking students, providing lunches and tutoring until the kids were finished with school and met the minimum qualifications for the armed services. "This made me feel there was indeed a poverty draft, something going on that was very unpleasant," she says. "I heard about the GI Rights Hotline from a neighbor, and it seemed like a good opportunity to help address the situation."

Soon a caller named Barbara is on the line, telling Zimmerman about her son Ian, who was inducted into the Army in April 2005 and started basic training as an infantryman. "There were certain things going on," Barbara starts her story carefully, "and when he tried to go to his superiors they just would laugh. He started getting scared."

Zimmerman encourages Barbara to continue.

"Kids who wouldn't score in marksmanship," Barbara reports, "they were just passing them anyway. That started to concern him. And then if he said anything about it, they were pretty aggressive with him."

Barbara says Ian asked the Army for an Entry Level Separation (ELS), a tool that the military uses to rid itself of recruits who prove to be unfit for duty. But the newly enlisted who decide that they've made a horrible mistake can use it for themselves if they can prove that they are unable to adapt to the military. Such a discharge carries no baggage; it's neither an honorable nor a dishonorable discharge. But the ELS must be requested during a recruit's first 180 days of continuous active-duty status.

"He just was laughed at," Barbara says about Ian's ELS request. So at the beginning of his eighth week of training, Ian jumped the fence and went AWOL. "He wants to get his discharge."

Zimmerman checks through her reference binders and begins to read Army regulations to Barbara: Once a soldier is AWOL for thirty days, the Army begins a process to officially declare him or her a deserter. When the paperwork arrives from the soldier's unit at a Fort Knox, Kentucky, office called the Deserter Information Point (USADIP in Army argot), AWOL status changes to deserter status. What is intriguing for those AWOL soldiers trying to work the system to their advantage is that they or a friend can call the USADIP to confirm that the soldier in question has achieved deserter status.[66] Deserters who are new to the Army and whose paperwork is in order at the DIP can surrender themselves. Those who do so tend to be thrown out of the service after a brief waiting period at either Fort Knox or Fort Sill, Oklahoma; they usually are offered an Other Than Honorable (OTH) discharge in lieu of a court-martial. The exact rules and policies differ among service branches.

"It's a good idea to call from a cell phone rather than a land line," Zimmerman advises Barbara, "because it doesn't reveal your exact location." [67]

"When they go to Fort Sill or Fort Knox," there's a mother's worry in Barbara's voice, "where do they keep them?"

Zimmerman pulls an e-mail printout off the wall and reads it to Barbara. It's from a GI whom the hotline helped through the deserter-to-discharge process. Excerpts from that – and a note from another deserter – help Zimmerman demystify for Barbara the series of events that can lead to severance from the service. When you arrive at Fort Sill and are checked in by the staff on duty, says the deserter's e-mail, the routine is simple:

> You will have to hand over any atm cards and forms of ID to be returned upon dismissal. Same goes for cd players, phones, over 20$ cash, etc. You will sign a few papers confirming your basic information, read your rights, then depending on what time it is, put

in with others. I was told to watch tv after I made my bed. . . . You can purchase sodas on free time, shower, read, tv, hang outside, etc. After about an hour I asked to use the phone. It is outside. I did this completely unsupervised. They aren't there to jail you, just to get you out.

The staff isn't there to prove to you how tough they are, they are fun to be around and they respect you like you are active duty. The details that you do during the day is minor cleanup and recycling, basically separating white from colored paper. The days can drag, but the weeks go quick. Just do what you are told, look busy at times that you need to, and you will be fine.

Barbara finds the first-person account from Fort Sill comforting. Zimmerman tells her that after Ian is declared a deserter, he will be listed as wanted on the national crime computer. "Anybody who is on the national crime computer has to be aware of that, and if they are picked up for jaywalking or a traffic violation, their name would come up. That's something he should consider." A deserter who gets arrested is more likely to face a court-martial and punishment than one who surrenders.

Zimmerman takes another call. Laura is on the line. She signed up for the Army under the Delayed Entry Program (DEP) and she wants out. "If you don't want to go through with it," she asks, "all you have to do is not show up? Is that right?"

"That's absolutely correct," says Zimmerman, but advises that a letter to the commanding officer of the recruiting station is not a bad idea. "Just say in the letter, 'I changed my mind.' And pretty much any reason will work. You can say you're going to school, you're getting married, you're going on a vacation, whatever. It's still a volunteer army and you are not in the military until you go for the second time to take the oath." Zimmerman is strident and deliberate with her advice. "Don't ever go back to the recruiting station for any reason. They'll tell you to come down and talk about it. Don't do it. There's no obligation for you to do that whatsoever. They figure if they can get you down there and either yell at you or sweet-talk you, they'll get you back. Don't go there."

"Okay," says Laura sweetly, her voice filled with relief. "Thank you so much!"

Steve Morse turned eighteen in 1964, before the serious escalation of the U.S. role in the Vietnam War. Raised a Quaker with a pacifist father, Morse enrolled in Swarthmore College and was promised conscientious objector classification from his draft board once he no longer qualified for a student deferment. At Swarthmore he joined Students for a Democratic Society and demonstrated against the war, before dropping out and eventually moving to California. He picketed the Oakland Induction Center and distributed antiwar newspapers to GIs, work that remarkably fulfilled the requirements for his alternative service.

Three months after completing his CO

requirements, in 1969, Morse joined the Army. In a soft and deliberate voice, he explains that seemingly counterintuitive decision with a simple, "That was a good place to try to help stop the war and build an overall movement." As far as he knows, he's the only CO in America who was so dedicated to his antiwar work that he joined the Army to lobby soldiers as a peer. After basic training at Fort Ord, Morse eventually shipped out to Cambodia and Vietnam with the 11th Armored Cavalry Regiment, organizing and resisting while trying to stay alive and remain true to his conscience.[68]

Now retired from a career that included sheet metal work and teaching math, Morse works full-time as program coordinator for the Oakland Central Committee for Conscientious Objectors office and takes his turns answering GI Rights Hotline calls. "We have people returning from the war who are slated to go back," Morse is describing a frequent type of caller. It's a problem that did not occur during the Vietnam War. Back then, completion of a tour of duty in the war zone guaranteed no return trip. "This is now the norm. Those people often call us when they're back, traumatized, gone AWOL."

In 2005, by the organization's count, an estimated 32,000 individual callers contacted the GI Rights Hotline; about 30 percent of those calls dealt with questions about being AWOL. For Morse, those 10,000 calls suggest that the Department of Defense announcement that some 5,500 military personnel are AWOL annually is likely a significant underestimate.

"All the sergeants know is to tell people to come back," Morse says about the military response to AWOL soldiers. The military does not want to publicize the fact that one route to discharge is by going AWOL. "That's the radical part of what we do," he says. "We can't advise people to go AWOL or advise them to stay AWOL. But we can give them this information – that there are certain ways to get out by going AWOL – and that's radical because the military won't do it." A growing percentage of calls to the hotline come from students who sign up for the Delayed Entry Program and then change their minds. "Recruiters are telling them they can't get out," says Morse, "and they can." Other calls come from soldiers traumatized by the Iraq War who want to apply for conscientious objector status. Accurate information is a critical component of the hotline work, because there's false information circulating as credible. "There are no conscientious objectors because there is no draft," I heard Rush Limbaugh crow to his millions of listeners on August 25, 2005. In fact, the military must accept CO requests from its members. After all, a conscience can be awakened by exposure to the realities of war.

"Basic training and boot camp are very psychologically invasive; they're designed to be," Morse says from intimate personal experience. Stories of training abuses and of the Iraq War fuel calls to the hotline about psychological crises. "The volunteer military is a misnomer. You volunteer at this one point and then the word volunteer ceases to be operative, unlike other aspects of life."

11

AIDAN DELGADO
The Buddhist Whistleblower

On the morning of September 11, 2001, unaware of the impending catastrophe, Aidan Delgado signed up for the Army Reserve. He was listless, unsure of his direction, frustrated with school, and looking for a different, more powerful challenge. Reserve duty two days a month sounded like an easygoing adventure to him. It wasn't until he'd signed the enlistment papers and was heading home that he heard of the attacks on the World Trade Center and the Pentagon. The result for Aidan was basic training and then transport to Iraq a year later with his unit, the 320th Military Police Company.

He spent six months working in Nasiriyah before being shipped to Abu Ghraib prison for another six months of duty. Not that the Middle East was foreign to him. He had spent considerable time during his grammar school days living in Cairo, where his father was employed by the U.S. Foreign Service. His conversational Arabic came in handy for his unit during street patrols in Nasiriyah.

"I would say I was a very atypical soldier; my opinions were definitely minority opinions," Aidan tells me on the telephone from Crawford, Texas. He's made the trip from his Florida home to support Cindy Sheehan, whose soldier son was killed in action in Iraq, and join her antiwar vigil outside President Bush's ranch.

Some of his childhood was spent in Thailand, and he points to a favorable impression of Buddhism that grew stronger as he matured. "After I enlisted in the Army I began to study Buddhism in earnest," he says. "After several weeks of intensive study and reflection, I had a light-bulb-over-the-head moment when I realized that Buddhism was something that I had always intuitively believed. It was more a discovery that I was a Buddhist than a conversion."

Nonetheless, Aidan acknowledges that even after what he calls his "Aha!" moment, he was not a very serious practitioner of the religion. "I found meditation extremely difficult and had not really made Buddhism a big part of my life." That changed while his military career progressed. "Over the next two years, I continued to read and study Buddhism, but more importantly I began to meditate and change things in my life that were no longer in line with my beliefs – things like violence and aggression. At the end of my AIT [Advanced Individual Training], I had become what I would consider a serious Buddhist, and this is when I began to strongly question my role in the military and whether I could continue to be a part of something that opposed my beliefs."

As soon as he filed for CO status, his relationships with his Army peers deteriorated. "My unit was immediately hostile against me. Guys in the unit wouldn't want to sit with me, wouldn't want to talk to me. My command took steps against me to make sure I was ostracized. It was a very difficult time for me. I was basically alone in my unit."

There were some exceptions. A mechanic, Aidan was assigned to the unit's motor pool. "The people in my motor pool who had worked with me personally remained very loyal to me, because they knew I was sincere, that I wasn't just trying to get out of it," he says. "People who didn't know me, like my commander, were the ones who were more hostile."

Aidan offers a litany of the punitive measures he faced. He says he was refused home leave while his CO application was pending, because the Army considered him a flight risk. He was ordered to relinquish his body armor, exposing him to great danger from incoming attacks targeting the compound. He believes these acts were designed to convince him to recant his opposition to the war. But as he witnessed or heard about abuses perpetrated against Iraqis by the U.S. military, he only became a more ardent opponent of U.S. policy and war as a policy tool.

I asked him the question so many pose about soldiers who oppose the war in Iraq: Isn't it a bit naïve or disingenuous to voluntarily join the military and then object to killing?

"They're always saying, 'Oh, you volunteered. You volunteered. This is what you volunteered for.' When a nineteen-year-old or an eighteen-year-old or a seventeen-year-old volunteers for something, they're an adult, but they're naïve. When I volunteered, and I think when most soldiers volunteer, they have the understanding that there is some kind of social compact that they will be used in a responsible way. When that trust is violated, in my opinion, the entire contract is morally nullified."

Aidan is not surprised so few soldiers are rejecting the mission in Iraq. "I think it's very easy to go along with the popular viewpoint and say, 'I support the war.' It's so easy to just be a hero. It takes an enormous amount of courage to break rank with virtually everyone in the military and take a stand." But he is quick to point out that not all those soldiers following orders believe the war is a good idea. "They just may not have the dedication or the determination to come out and make a public statement." He says he now meets soldiers who tell him that they support his stance against the war but remain clandestine about their point of view because they fear reprisals from the military.

Aidan says the transformation for him began a couple of months after he arrived in Iraq. "Working with prisoners in Nasiriyah really began to work on my conscience and work on my mind. When I saw the human face of my enemy, or who was supposed to be my enemy – that I found to be very touching and very enlightening. I felt their humanity. That was what really began to make me question my own morals and take a stand on what I believed, the face-to-face contact."

That contact reinforced his faith and helped convince him that his interpretation of Buddhism meant he was a pacifist. "In almost every Buddhist sect," Aidan wrote to me in an e-mail after our phone conversation, "nonviolence and inner peace are absolutely center stage. Buddhism condemns war, violence, and hatred of every kind." He offered his theory of why some casual observers of the religion may think otherwise. "Many people believe that Buddhism does not teach pacifism because of the strong influence of Zen Buddhism on the samurai culture of Japan. The popular impression of samurai imagery has led many people to believe that one could be a 'warrior Buddhist' or a 'Zen warrior.'" Not so, he insists, even though he admits that when he first called himself a Buddhist he bought into much of the warrior Buddhist mythology.

"This is a misunderstanding," he noted. "Even at the time, the samurai class of Japan was definitely outside the mainstream teachings of Buddhism. Medieval Japanese warriors used Zen meditation and focus techniques to improve their warrior skills, but they never accepted the ethical or compassionate aspects of Buddhism. Duty always came first. In effect, the Zen Buddhism of popular samurai culture was an abridged and debased form of Buddhism that was very different from anything else being practiced at the time or historically. True Buddhism is absolutely unequivocal on the subject of warfare and killing. The first precept of Buddhism (one of the five ethical rules akin to the Ten Commandments in Christianity) is 'Do not take life.' This is probably the only hard rule in Buddhism."

Aidan's story was prominently told by Bob Herbert on the *New York Times*'s op-ed page on May 2, 2005, in a column subtitled, "A Soldier Recoils as Civilians Abused." Herbert wrote that Aidan told him American soldiers routinely inflicted gratuitous violence on ordinary Iraqis. "Guys in my unit," he quoted Aidan, "particularly the younger guys, would drive by in their Humvee and shatter bottles over the heads of Iraqi civilians passing by. They'd keep a bunch of empty Coke bottles in the Humvee to break over people's heads." Herbert listed other abuses Aidan told him he'd witnessed: an Army sergeant whipping children with a radio antenna, a Marine corporal kicking a young child in the chest.

One incident that stands out among Aidan's ghastly stories occurred during a demonstration by prisoners against living conditions at Abu Ghraib prison. "There were almost these continual nightly demonstrations. The prisoners would march around in the yard, protesting," he told host Amy Goodman on a December 17, 2004, broadcast of *Democracy Now*. Aidan's unit was sent to help restore order. He stayed behind at the motor-pool garage. He'd already filed for CO status and had turned in his weapons; he refused to participate in any fighting and was not invited. But he heard what happened next when his unit returned from the action. "They were throwing tent stakes and pieces of stone and debris. They had struck one of the soldiers with a rock. He wasn't seriously injured, but he was annoyed. In response, they had asked to use lethal force. They opened fire with a heavy machine gun and they killed five prisoners – several of whom took several days to die. This is something I heard from the horse's mouth when they came back and told me." Aidan says the killings were documented by photographs snapped by soldiers in his unit, photographs he says his command posted in his unit's headquarters as trophies.

Herbert wrote that Aidan confronted a sergeant who had fired on the detainees. Herbert's column concludes: " 'I asked him,' said Mr. Delgado, 'if he was proud that he had shot unarmed men behind barbed wire for throwing stones. He didn't get mad at all. He was, like, 'Well, they bloodied my buddy's nose, so I knelt down. I said a prayer. I stood up, and I shot them down.' "

Aidan's charges and Herbert's credibility immediately were attacked in the blogosphere. The blog Blackfive.net sought reaction from its readers by posting excerpts from Herbert's column with the comment, "I was annoyed by this obvious slander and Delgado discussing physical abuse without any corroboration. Couldn't Mr. Herbert have found someone who also was there to confirm these accusations of abuse?" Blackfive then posted a link to the blog "Been There, Done That,"[69] written by the anonymous SGT Ted, who said that he was present at the Abu Ghraib riot in question: "The riot was also an escape attempt. It wasn't just a few stone throwers. . . . The stones being thrown represented a deadly force threat. . . . It was only when the riot became a danger of a serious breakout attempt . . . was the request for deadly force made. When permission was granted, two soldiers fired on the ring leaders. 3 were killed outright, ending the riot immediately. . . . I know both of the soldiers who fired; they are good people and only did what they had to do to keep others from further harm."

This and other blogs and their long lists of attacks against Aidan's credibility come up high on a Google search of his name.

"It's wild," Aidan said to me from Crawford about the blog attacks. "It was very hurtful to me, because [the Herbert column] was my first foray into the mainstream media. I really wasn't prepared for it. I didn't like it when strangers were questioning my integrity. But now that I have a little more experience, I really see it for what it was. It's a pattern of the right wing, and I think the media, to give these ad hominem attacks. They're doing them right now with Cindy Sheehan. The whole gist of their strategy is, don't attack the message, attack the messenger. So they can say I'm a communist or I'm trying to bring down America, and not try and confront the message, which is: We did this and I have pictures of it. I have pictures of U.S. soldiers posing with the corpses of people that they killed for protesting living conditions. That is unarguable. It's a fact. But they can try and undermine me, and I think that's what they did. They're all kind of on the same page, coordinating that effort."

Despite the criticism, Aidan continues to speak wherever he can draw a crowd. "This was so morally abhorrent to me," Aidan said to me about the killings during his tour of duty at Abu Ghraib, "this was like the final straw."

Aidan received an honorable discharge as a conscientious objector once his unit returned to the States. "I had a lot of witnesses from my unit testify on my behalf." He hopes to go to law school and is considering a career in politics. "Iraq," he says, "activated me. And now that I'm on, I can't really turn myself off. I want to keep up the fight."

12

OTHER REJECTIONISTS

The roll call of soldiers who now oppose, or at least question, the Iraq War that they were sent to fight keeps growing. Some are now well-known figures, such as Private Jessica Lynch. Wounded by regular Iraqi troops during the initial invasion, held prisoner, and finally rescued by U.S. forces, Lynch was portrayed by the Bush administration as a hero early in the war. By the time she told her own story, her summary was precise. "We went and we did our job, and that was to go to the war, but I wish I hadn't done it – I wish it had never happened. I wish we hadn't been there, none of us." Sitting in a wheelchair in her family's West Virginia kitchen, she told reporter Rick Bragg, the author of her authorized biography, "I don't care about the political stuff. But if it had never happened, Lori [a fellow soldier killed when Jessica's convoy was ambushed] would be alive and all the rest of the soldiers would be alive. And none of this," Bragg reports she was referring to her scars and need for a wheelchair, "would have happened." [70] By 2005, Lynch was walking with a cane and a leg brace and was enrolled at West Virginia University.

Arizona Cardinals football star Pat Tillman famously dismissed a multiyear, multimillion-dollar contract with the team and instead joined the Army after the 9/11 attacks. He was sent to fight first in Iraq and then in Afghanistan. His enlistment was a public relations bull's-eye for the Bush administration, one they took advantage of a second time when he was shot dead while on patrol in Afghanistan. The Pentagon initially announced he died a hero in combat with the enemy, and President Bush called him "an inspiration who made the ultimate sacrifice in the War on Terror." Five weeks later, the military acknowledged that he was killed by "friendly fire." A soldier who was near Tillman when he was shot down, Specialist Russell Baer, had also served with him in Iraq. Baer told *San Francisco Chronicle* reporter Robert Collier that Tillman was opposed to the Iraq war from the start. "We were . . . watching as bombs were dropping on the town," Baer said. "We weren't in the fight right then. We were talking. And Pat said, 'You know, this war is so f – – – illegal.' That's who he was. He totally was against Bush." [71]

Camilo Mejía spent six months fighting in Iraq, an experience that convinced him the war was illegal and immoral. During home leave in 2004, he told the Army he refused to return to duty in Iraq and instead filed as a conscientious objector – the first Iraq War veteran to do so. The sergeant surrendered to the military. He was denied CO status, sentenced to a year in prison for desertion, and given a bad-conduct discharge. "I had to come forward to speak for soldiers who were opposed to the war – soldiers who are fighting a corporate war," [72] he said over and over during speeches around the country following his release from prison.

Sergeant Kevin Benderman, another antiwar cause celebre, was convicted by a military court of "missing movement by design" and sentenced to fifteen months in prison and a dishonorable discharge. After serving ten years in the Army, including a tour of duty in Iraq, the forty-year-old Benderman applied for CO status, explaining, "I went to war. I never ran from it. I experienced it and I realized it's not what I should be doing. In my opinion, it's not what anybody should be doing in the modern world."[73] With Benderman behind bars at Fort Lewis, Washington, Amnesty International labeled him a "prisoner of conscience" and called for his immediate and unconditional release. The human rights group urged its members to send appeals to President Bush.[74] From his prison cell, Benderman wrote weekly letters to supporters continuing his politicking against the war, such as this one:

> It has been said that you should never question what the heads of government tell you is right, but I say that by the very way that the constitution of this country is laid out there is an expectation of every citizen to do just that.
>
> It is every citizen's responsibility, as well as their inherent right, to question the motives of our elected leaders. Our form of government is unique in the world in that respect. Slowly we have allowed those that we have hired to serve us in our government to twist the intent of the founding fathers into

what we now have. They now want us to believe that we are never supposed to question their actions or hold them accountable for the mistakes they make. And yet, in certain cases, there are actions that they take which are blatantly illegal. I believe it is past time for the citizens of this country to stand up and tell the people we have hired to work for us that we expect them to perform to the higher standard we have set for them.[75]

Carl Webb served seven years in the Army and then enlisted in the Texas Army National Guard. Two weeks before his Guard service was scheduled to end, Webb became a victim of the military's "stop-loss program," which allows the armed forces to suspend retirement and other scheduled discharges for soldiers during times of war and other national emergencies. It is, essentially, a military draft for those already in the service – soldiers who volunteered for the military with an expectation of a specific limited term of service. Webb, at the age of thirty-nine, had his military service involuntarily extended and was ordered to serve in a tank company near Baghdad.

Webb refused the order and went AWOL. But unlike many AWOL soldiers, he didn't go completely underground. On the contrary, he built a website to lobby against the Iraq War. "Most soldiers obey their orders because they are afraid of what could happen to them," says Webb. "They think, 'Oh, they are going to throw me in a dungeon, and put shackles on me, and I'll never see the light of day,' or they fear the isolation. . . . But just by being out there, I am going to give them ideas. I'm an example."[76] As of late 2005 the Army had yet to catch up with Carl Webb.

When Specialist Blake LeMoine sought CO status at his base in Germany after serving in Iraq, he called the military enlistment contract "a slave contract" because of the stop-loss provision, and he refused to obey any further orders.[77] "It is very much like a roach motel," LeMoine said about the Army at a news conference. "People check in, but they can't check out."[78] The Army saw things differently and sentenced LeMoine to seven months in prison.

Another public example is Rob Sarra, an organizer with Iraq Veterans Against the War. He was a Marine Corps sergeant in 2003, serving in al-Shatra, on patrol against the growing number of suicide bombers attacking U.S. forces. An old woman was walking toward his unit, carrying something. The Marines demanded she stop, but she kept coming. "I was looking at her, and I thought, 'I have to stop this woman.'" It's a story he keeps reliving. "So I fired on her, and then the other Marines fired on her. When we got to her, we saw she was pulling out a white flag. She had tea and bread in her bag. I kept thinking, 'Was she a grandmother? Was she a mother?'"[79] The woman was dead; Sergeant Sarra became one more post-traumatic stress disorder victim.

Tim Predmore, thirty-six, on active duty with the 101st Airborne near Mosul in 2003, sent a letter to his hometown newspaper, the *Peoria* (Illinois) *Journal*

Star. "This looks like a modern-day crusade not to free an oppressed people or to rid the world of a demonic dictator relentless in his pursuit of conquest and domination, but a crusade to control another nation's natural resource," Predmore wrote. "I no longer believe; I have lost my conviction, my determination. I can no longer justify my service for what I believe to be half-truths and bold lies. We have all faced death here without reason or justification."[80]

Staff Sergeant Mike Parrot was shot dead while on patrol in Iraq for the Pennsylvania National Guard. "I've lost my best friend, and I don't know what life will be like without him," said Meg Corwin of her 49-year-old husband. And then she added this despairing coda to his death: "My husband and I both loathe and despise the war. He was under no illusion about this war. He didn't believe the Bush administration's reasons for the war, but he believed he could do some good."[81]

Army Specialist Marquise Roberts took a different route out of Iraq. He was accused of convincing a cousin to shoot him in the leg while he was on leave in Philadelphia in December 2004. "I was scared," he told police. "I didn't want to go back to Iraq and leave my family. I felt that my chain of command didn't care about the safety of the troops. I just know that I was not going to make it back."[82]

Another serviceman who apparently drafted a cousin to help him stay out of Iraq was Marine Moises Hernandez, who faced the felony charge of filing a false police report in Chicago after allegedly convincing his cousin to shoot him in the leg, an injury he reported as the result of random gang gunfire. His father said Hernandez's experiences in Iraq caused him nightmares and "changed him totally."[83]

The first soldier to object to the Iraq War by filing a CO application was Marine Lance Corporal Stephen Funk. He refused to deploy when his unit shipped out to Iraq, went AWOL, and worked with his lawyer finishing the CO application paperwork. The week the fighting started, Stephen turned himself in to the Marines after calling a news conference and explaining that he had learned just before he received orders for Iraq that conscientious objection is an option for soldiers. "That's one of the reasons I'm going public with this," he told reporters. "I think this generation going into combat doesn't even know about it. I'd like to let people know there's an option."[84]

Before Stephen was convicted of "unauthorized absence" – the Marine Corps terminology for AWOL – and served six months in the Camp Lejeune brig, he made his position clear. "I refuse to kill," he said simply.[85] "In writing my application for discharge, I was completely honest about who I am. Part of that meant acknowledging that I am gay. I believe that homosexuals should be able to serve if they choose, and that Don't Ask Don't Tell is an awful policy that only helps the military perpetuate anti-gay sentiment among its ranks. However, I am not an advocate for gay inclusion in the military because I personally do not support military action."[86]

Two weeks before he was due to be mustered out of the Army, I talked with a relieved Steven Casey, a soldier who was disgusted with the duty he'd been ordered to perform during his fifteen months in Iraq, convinced by his experiences that the Iraq War was illegal, and certain he would never fight for the U.S. Army again. When we met near his base in Germany, he relived the raids on Iraqi houses he and his unit conducted.

"You break their door down," he says, telling me about the same type of assignment Joshua Key was forced to perform. "You go in their house and you look for soft spots in the walls. If you feel a soft spot, you break a hole in the wall. You use sledgehammers to break down doors and walls." The raids were conducted in the middle of the night. "You go in their house, you completely disrupt their house, all their drawers are inside out." The occupants are crying and screaming. "We tear things up, things that they probably can't afford to fix. Broken mirrors. You're throwing stuff around trying to find things."

On a jerky and dark videotape Steven shot during one of the raids, I listen to the audio track as the soldiers – their voices pumped with adrenalin – bark out orders that sound understandably fearful and demanding at the same time.

From one voice is the call, "All right, Team One, let's go! Team Two, come back!"

A second voice yells at the occupants, "Get out! Get out! Get out! Get out!"

Then a third soldier: "Stay outside!"

It's chaos as a woman's voice, in accented English, pleads, terrified, "What's happened?" And then, "My children! My children! What's happened?" She cries out over and over, "What? What?"

And from the soldiers, running footfalls and "Let's go! Let's go!"

The confusion is clear in the cacophony of soldiers' voices:

"What the fuck are you doing?"

"Bust this fucking lock down. Let's go! Let's go!"

"Got your hammer? Bust this lock open!"

"Where's the sledge?"

"You fucking just had it in your hand!"

"Get the sledge, man. Let's go!"

"What the fuck? Did you see the sledge?"

"First floor, first floor!"

More footsteps as the sledgehammer is retrieved.

"Bust the fucking lock open!"

The repeated dull thud of the hammer on the lock.

Finally, "Fucking nothing."

Steven says they ransacked the places in as orderly a fashion as they could, but they were also working as fast as possible. "'Go in and get out,' they tell you, but you have to make sure it's thorough. You're flipping up the mattresses, you're taking out the drawers. [Local custom dictates that] you're not supposed to touch a married woman's anything. We're going through her underwear, throwing her shirts around. For the rest of her life she'll never forget this; she's ruined. And for what? It was the wrong house. It's a 'dry hole' is the phrase they use," he says about his superiors, and he apologizes for the crude Army slang. "It's a dry hole for us, for the rest of her life this lady is emotionally damaged." His voice gets quiet – just above a whisper – as he says, "I can't do things like that anymore for no reason."

He'll still be liable for a call back if the Army decides it needs him. "I'm susceptible for the next five years to the Inactive Reserves. These guys can call me up anytime. But I won't come back."

"What will happen if they call you back?"

"You'll see me on the news. I won't be back. I'll be a statistic of a guy who doesn't show up." Again his voice is quiet as he says again, "I'm not coming back." Steven says he's going to college when he gets home, an education he'll pay for with the money the Army guaranteed him when he enlisted. "I did get what I was promised," he says about his benefits package. "I got everything they said I was going to get. I got a hunk of money for school, and with that I got social anxiety and I got this cool skin rash that I'm never going to get rid of. I've got a social disorder. I yell at my wife. I don't think I won. There are a lot of things that came with this that are irreparable and I'm going to have the rest of my life." He talks about anger and anxiety. He wonders if he's suffering from post-traumatic stress disorder, if he's facing a lifetime of prescription drugs and psychiatrists. "I know it wasn't any Vietnam, but it got me somehow. I wish I could make it all go away, to be honest with you. But I can't. I should have worked at McDonald's and found a way to pay for my tuition."

Steven talks about his friends who finished college

while he was serving in the Army. He says he feels as if his life has been on pause.

"I'm not giving up my school to go do this again – an unjustified war for these evil people. I'll go to jail. I don't care. I'm not going back. Jail is not something you want to have on your record, but neither is unjustified murder. I would rather go to jail and not kill anyone than to go over there and have a chance to kill an innocent person again. It's not going to happen. I'll do anything not to go back." Now his voice gets louder and stronger. "I'm not going back to work for these people. I've been to war. I was an eighteen-year-old kid who went to war. I'm done."

And for what?

13

CLIFTON HICKS
"I'll Be Home Soon"

We're sitting at the Holiday Inn in Heidelberg, Germany, just before the Heidelberg Volksfest, and Clifton Hicks is telling me some horrific tales from his time in Iraq. The son and grandson of soldiers, Clifton was not yet nineteen when he found himself working as a gunner on a Humvee on the dusty roads of Baghdad.

"The first time that I really saw some shit go down that really freaked me out, we were driving around at night," he begins to tell me. "There were all these packs of wild dogs all over Baghdad, they chased the Humvees, and they yipped and yapped. This one night the headlights went over a pack of dogs and they're eating something. They were eating a couple of dead people that had been picked down to the rib cage. I was eighteen and a half, had never even been to a funeral before, had never killed anything other than a raccoon or a possum, get grossed out going to a butcher's market or a fish store.

"And here I'm seeing a rib cage, bare. And a bunch of dogs eating it."

For Clifton, being in the Army was the fulfillment of a childhood dream. Born in Jacksonville, Florida, he grew up in Tampa and Savannah before moving back to Tampa when his parents divorced. In early

2003, armed with a high school diploma he earned via correspondence courses, he joined the Army. He always wanted to "be a tanker," to drive a tank and fight in a war. He expected to enjoy a military career as a lifer, through to retirement.

Just weeks after graduating from basic training at Fort Knox, Clifton shipped out to Germany, where he "received some ramshackle training." A couple of weeks later he was on a plane to Kuwait, and then was sent on to Iraq. Within a few more weeks he was driving Humvees and tanks on patrol, and working as a gunner on Humvees. "I didn't know how to use the weapon yet – the machine gun," he says. "But they had me up there gunning on it. I learned pretty quick." For the next ten months he was a gunner on a Humvee and a tank driver in the 1st Squadron, 1st U.S. Cavalry Regiment. "Most of the time I was just standing on the gunner's hatch of a Humvee, looking back and forth."

The duty was mostly a dismal routine for Clifton. "We'd go out and nine days out of ten you'd just be sitting up there and it'd be raining," he recalls. "You'd drive through these flooded streets, and get shit-splashed – literally – I'm talking about shit water with people walking through it. It'd splash in your face and your eyes, and you get sick from it. You're covered in human feces. You're sitting around just bored and miserable, wishing you weren't there. You sing a song or you talk to yourself. Make fun of each other. Let your mind wander. Fall asleep standing up. I would volunteer for night missions. The most dangerous job for a gunner would be a night mission on the tail

Humvee. The Humvees go out in pairs, one in front with a guy standing in front, and one in back with a guy watching over the rear. I'd volunteer to that. It was the most dangerous job, nobody wanted to do it. I would do that at night just so I could go to sleep. I would sit up there on the gun and sleep standing up, the whole four hours. Most of the time it was pure boredom, but every once in a while. . . ."

Seeing the dogs picking at the human rib cage is clearly among his many vivid memories. Clifton looks drawn as we talk; his eyes are piercing when he tells his war stories, as if he is reliving the moments he's describing.

Outside, Heidelberg's perfectly preserved Renaissance neighborhoods bustle with activity in the shadow of its magnificent castle overlooking the Neckar River. Posters for the fair are spotted all around the storybook-looking city, decorated with the American flag and including the English line, WITH A TASTE OF AMERICA, plus the promise, in the hyphenated German style, of the US-ARMY-BAND.

Heidelberg, long a U.S. Army headquarters city and home to one of Germany's important universities, is accustomed to Americans in its midst. Clifton is stationed a couple of hours drive north, in Büdingen, "a one-horse town, just a horrible place," he says.

During much of Clifton's Iraq tour, the scene was calm when he was on patrol. It was after the initial invasion and before the insurgency developed into a consequential threat to U.S. forces. "There were occasional poorly made explosives on the side of the road; you could usually spot them and get rid of them," he says. "Occasionally some guy would get drunk and decide he wanted to shoot us. He'd go up on his roof and he'd ra-tat-ta-ta-ta-ta-da, and run away. It was like being a police officer in a really bad neighborhood."

Clifton is a good storyteller, and his tough GI lexicon mixes freely with a sophisticated interpretation of his ten months in Iraq. His speech is staccato as he recounts one of the first events that began to turn him against the war.

"We were driving around one night in the Humvees in Baghdad, nothing out of the ordinary," he begins. "We got out there and immediately this drunk guy got pissed off and threw something at the Humvee. I thought it was a hand grenade at first. I was just about to shoot this guy. It was a bottle and broke on the back of the Humvee. I was not going to shoot this guy for throwing a bottle. I was kind of shaken from that."

The patrol continued. And things got worse. "We heard a lot of gunfire up ahead and you could tell it wasn't just a couple AK-47s, it was some U.S. weapons firing back," he recounts. "We knew somebody was in a fight up there. We race ahead down the street and there's an 82nd Airborne infantry platoon and they're all parked in their Humvees – about four Humvees packed with guys. There's a house with the lights on and people are all around the place. There's a big fuss going on.

"We pull up and we say, 'What's going on? We heard some shooting up here.' And they're like, 'Yeah, we got ambushed just now.' They started clearing buildings to find out who was firing at them. They kicked in this first door and there's a wedding party going on. What they do in Baghdad, when there's a wedding, they shoot into the air. These people were up on their roof, probably a little sauced up, happy there's a wedding, and I guess Grandpa is up on the roof shooting off his rifle at the same time as this 82nd patrol drives by and is engaged by insurgents from a field. They returned fire in both directions, and I think most of them returned fire on the wedding party. They returned fire on the wedding party and they shot three people, three people at a wedding party. Because somebody was shooting into the air to celebrate, these guys wanted to kill him."

Clifton watched as soldiers searched the field for the enemy and found nothing but some AK-47 shell casings. "The insurgents were fine, not a scratch on them. They made it just fine. The innocent people who were partying, just trying to celebrate a wedding, three of them had been shot. One man had been shot in the arm, a girl had been shot in the leg, and one younger girl who was about six was dead – laying on the ground, dead. She was six years old, laying on the ground, face down, palms up, in a little flowery dress. She was stone dead. Mothers and women are all bawling and crying. The men are all standing in shock. We bandaged up the one guy. The one little girl was crying, she was maybe ten, shot in the leg. Everyone is sitting around like, 'Yeah, they fucking killed some little kid.' I'm like, 'What the fuck? That's pretty shitty.'

"The 82nd called it up to their guys and their command said, 'Charlie Mike [military parlance for "Continue the mission"], just keep going.' They packed up and drove off. So we just hopped in our Humvees and we drove off too.

"And that was the end of it. They applied first aid to the people who had been shot. The girl who was dead, they just left her there on the floor. We drove off and continued the mission."

Clifton looks shell-shocked in the Holiday Inn lobby as he tells the story, distraught and puzzled and disturbed all at the same time. "Continue the mission? I was like, 'What the fuck is that all about?' We're supposed to be here to rebuild this country, to help these people, and we just shot three people. We just killed somebody's daughter. And we drove off. That's never going to be reported in the news. No one is ever going to know about it except people who were there."

The dead girl was the beginning of Clifton's epiphany. After just a few months in the midst of the post-invasion Iraq, he began to question the war. He became convinced the U.S. policy was counterproductive. He saw his role as a waste of time, and he decided to simply work at staying alive until he completed his Iraq tour of duty. He read books sent from home, kept up his diary, and sent some plaintive e-mails: "Please write and let me know what's going on around home. I'm always worrying in the back of my mind that I'll return home to find everything dramatically changed; that everyone hates me and I've been disowned or some crap."

Finally, departure day arrived for his squadron. They loaded the tanks onto flatbed trucks and drove south to Kuwait. "We crossed the border. The first tank that crossed, they started cheering. And then the next tank cheers. The whole convoy is just screaming and yelling. We're like, 'Yeah! We got the fuck out of there!' We're in Kuwait. We're safe. We can put our weapons down because no one is going to kill us in Kuwait."

The euphoria was short-lived. They enjoyed the relative luxury of the base – "There's a Subway, there's a Baskin-Robbins, there's a damn Pizza Hut, there's a swimming pool," reports Clifton – as they prepared their gear for the trip back to their home base in Germany. But it was April 2004, and security in Iraq was deteriorating fast. U.S. forces were struggling in their attempts to contain the growing violent opposition to their occupation. Clifton and the 1-1 Cav were ordered back to Iraq.

It was a brutal time, and Clifton wrote home with details:

> 135 of our soldiers were killed in April. One of them was a Staff Sergeant who I had met in Germany. We flew into Iraq together side by side on the same C-130. At one point the crew noticed that a guided missile had been fired at us and we all hung on for dear life as the plane banked left and right, discharging its anti SAM [shoulder-to-air missile] thermal flares in a thankfully successful attempt to save our hides.
>
> Staff Sergeant "R" was on top of his tank

getting an MRE and some water for his loader (who happened to be a good friend of mine from basic training) when they came under attack. Haj shot an RPG at them, the rocket missed the tank, but it hit SSG. "R" square in the chest and split him right down the middle. The loader (who's name and rank I won't mention at all) jumped up on the loader's M240 and fired into a crowd of civilians who were standing there, killing and maiming a large number of them. He told me that he just "freaked out," I guess he didn't know what else to do.

I myself saw a number of people killed and wounded in Iraq. All but one of them were unarmed Iraqis. The one guy who could be considered an "enemy combatant" blew his own hand off trying to hang mortar rounds on us, but besides him they were all innocent as far as I know. Sometimes they got shot, sometimes they got run over by humvees or tanks. Sometimes they were just laying there dead and nobody knew what had killed them.

The military doesn't like Clifton Hicks and Clifton Hicks doesn't like the military. That became clear to both sides when Clifton's father posted one of his letters home on the family's blog, where his commanders read it carefully. It was April 2004 when Clifton's fingers flew over the keyboard and punched SEND after composing a diatribe.

First, he described how his unit was in Kuwait

after their tour of duty in Iraq, waiting to go home, when they were sent back to Iraq to quell uprisings. Morale, Clifton said, had "plummeted from 'pretty low' to 'non-existent.'" His "elite" unit was the QRF (quick reaction force), which meant whenever "they've got some dirty work, we have to go there."

Then Clifton's note revealed some shocking details:

> Just got out of some miserable town that had been blown to pieces, 700-900 dead (all "enemies" right?). The battle was over and the bodies cleaned up by the time we got there. It's like being invited to a party when it's already over and when you get there the guy who invited you says, "Here, I need you to clean up all these beer cans for me. Somebody puked in the bathroom too, and can you mow my grass when you're done?" Fuck you General Abizaid.[87] There were a lot of dead cows and horses that we used to zero our weapons, and I ran over a couple cars (on purpose this time). Everyone is so pissed about this stupid crap that they just want to get the anger out. We'd like spit in the President's face, and tell all the Generals to go fuck themselves, but we can't do that (because the damn cowards aren't here) so instead we take it out on (most likely) innocent Iraqis. Running over cars, or even throwing trash on the side of the road makes you feel good. It's really fun to take a shit in an MRE [Meals Ready to Eat] bag and

throw it out to the people who are begging for food, who then fight over it. That's not even the worst that I've seen or done. The whole thing is disgusting.

So basically that's all we're doing. They sent us back to help fix Iraq, but all any of us are doing is trying to have fun, mostly at the expense of the country we are supposed to be helping. Congratulations you stupid Generals, what an excellent plan. I guess I sound really bitter and pissed off, and I guess I am, but now I've progressed past that, I've detached myself, because that's the only way you can get by without losing it and doing something stupid. We had a platoon meeting today and they told us about our new mission and how much it was going to suck, everyone else looked like they'd just seen Old Yeller bite the dust but I was smiling because me and Slater were going to watch The Goonies (for the second night in a row) on his DVD player afterwards. I've learned to pay more attention to the simple pleasures rather than the complex miseries which occupy my current existence. There's no sense in being miserable about it, I was depressed for a few days, was even thinking about shooting a hole through my foot or something stupid like that, but it passed.

Anyhow, it's almost midnight here and I've got about a mile hike to get home so I must be going. Please send me mail!

Once Clifton's Army commanders read that letter, he suffered a Field Grade Article 15, charged with OPSEC – operations security – violations and disrespecting officials and superior commissioned officers, which, he says, "nearly landed me in jail for treason and dishonorably discharged."

He woke up one morning as his commanding officers kicked his cot. "They told me to get the fuck up. They had this big stack of papers in front of me with my name all over it." It was material from the blog, criticism of the military and the mission. "Stuff I had written. They read the whole thing to me." He acknowledged that the words were his. "They were going to throw me in jail for treason. They were going to kick me out of the Army." Instead he lucked out with a slap: demotion to private, a fine of some eight hundred dollars, and a couple of months' extra duty. His response to the punishments was to file for CO status.

Clifton survived the redeployment, and once back in Germany he filed an AR 600-43, his official application to be discharged from the Army as a conscientious objector. His statement on the form was succinct: "It is against my moral and religious beliefs to take human life under any circumstances; I am opposed to war in any form. As long as I live, I will never attempt to kill another living person. I am seeking classification as a conscientious objector and separation from the military."

The form requires the applicant to explain how his beliefs changed or developed, and Clifton noted his deadly experiences in Iraq, such as the inadvertent assault on the wedding party. He detailed an event when his patrol in Baghdad came under fire. "I identified where the firing was coming from and returned fire, the enemy firing stopped immediately and nothing more became of it, the incident was never reported. This was a major turning point in my life, I was thoroughly repulsed by what I had done and prayed that I would never have to try to kill a fellow human being again."

Clifton summed up his position with a preemptive written strike against any critics who would dismiss his CO application as a device to attempt an early discharge from the Army. "There are those who remain skeptical of my claims; I am thought of by some of my superiors as a liar, an idiot, and a coward. They and those who think alike are entitled to their beliefs, just as I am entitled to mine. If only they knew how much honesty, intelligence and courage it takes to pursue such beliefs, thus enduring the persecution and hatred of such a multitude of naysayers. My actions in the past and at present have well proven that I am not a coward, for a coward will never do what he believes to be right when those around him say that he is wrong, he will simply be bullied into submission. I expect that none of us would have found ourselves in disagreement with Abraham Lincoln when he said, 'To sin by silence when they should protest makes cowards of men.' I intend to live my own life in a way that will affirm the lives of others, not destroy them."

Not that Clifton was counting on the Army to approve his CO application. "If I don't get it? I have other avenues of approach to get home," he tells me. "I've told them I am not going to go back to Iraq." He says he'd rather go to prison than back to the war. "It won't come to that, though, because I think I'm too smart for that to happen to me. Civil disobedience is an option – just refuse to put the uniform on. Maybe a hunger strike. There's all kinds of things you can do. It's looking like they'll approve it. But if they don't, I have Plan B, Plan C, all the way up to desertion."

He exhibits calm about his circumstances. He's made up his mind. "It's not that I won't go back," he says about Iraq, "it's that I *can't* go back. I just hate that place so much. The sad thing is that I hate those people. I hate the reason we're there." He's spitting the words out now. "The whole place is just so foul. It's a cesspool of pure evil. The insurgents are evil, but we're evil too. The insurgent who's killing me, he's being used just like I am. They say these guys are mindless – look at us. Shit, we joined up too. We're both volunteers fighting each other. Once we volunteer, we can't leave. We become conscripts. We're just pawns. We're being used."

It's a war, says Clifton Hicks, fought for "filthy rich bastards too cowardly to do it themselves" who want more money, fought by "us, the masses of uneducated fools killing each other."

Early in November 2005, I received a celebratory e-mail from Clifton. "I just found out that my [CO] application has been approved and I've been recommended for honorable discharge by the

Commanding General." The note starts out like a dry recitation of the facts, with no emotion. "So I'm good to go I guess," and he adds, "I'll be home soon." And then a line of understated reflection, "It's been a really tough period in my life." And finally a cry of relief, "I nearly fell over like a sack of potatoes when they gave me the news, I could hardly contain myself!"

EPILOGUE
What Happened to Them Next?

As of January 2006, here are the updates on the soldiers profiled in this book:

After a family road trip across Canada, **Joshua Key** and his wife, Brandi, decided they liked bucolic British Columbia better than city life in Toronto. They settled on Gabriola Island, where Joshua was waiting for the Canadian Immigration and Refugee Board to hear his case.

At last report, **Ryan Johnson** also was waiting for the Canadian government to act on his request to stay in the country. He and his wife, Jennifer, continued to find the bright lights of Toronto a welcome change from their sleepy California hometown.

Once **Clara Gomez** mustered the strength to reject the Army, she went back to school, intent on maintaining a high grade point average en route to her college degree.

Still waiting for the Veterans Administration to change its bureaucratic ruling and provide him with benefits so that he can get treatment for his combat-induced post-traumatic stress disorder, **Daniel** was last reported looking for work, anxious to do an honest day of work for a fair paycheck.

Robert Zabala faithfully kept showing up for duty as a Marine Reservist, patiently waiting for the Corps to award him conscientious objector status while he pursued his studies at the University of California.

Pleased with his conscientious objector discharge, **Aidan Delgado** hit the antiwar lecture circuit and wrote a book about his experiences as a soldier in Iraq.

Clifton Hicks celebrated the Army decision to relieve him of duty as a conscientious objector and headed home to visit family in South Carolina and Florida, the war still with him. "Just today," he wrote to me on December 19, 2005, "I was walking in the woods with my dad and my foot got tangled up in a thin vine. I yanked my foot free and immediately thought of how stupid I was to tug at something like that, which might be a trip wire. Then I remembered that people don't generally booby-trap deer trails in South Carolina."

ACKNOWLEDGMENTS

Who to thank for all the help I was fortunate enough to receive while working on this project? High on the list, of course, are all the soldiers who shared their stories with me. There would be no *Mission Rejected* without them.

As always is the case with my work, I've been saved from myself by the ruthless first-round editing of the manuscript by my wife, the writer Sheila Swan Laufer. My professional and personal debts to her are infinite. My sons, Talmage and Michael, fueled my work on this project with their own rejection of the military and their activism against war. The memory of my parents, and the guidance and support they provided me during the Vietnam War era, were always present while I researched, reported, and wrote.

I received critical research support from my friend and colleague Robert Simmons; particularly important was his work at the Veterans for Peace conference near Dallas. Other friends and colleagues – George Papagiannis, André Spears, and Terry Phillips – offered valuable critiques of some early drafts. My periodic partner in journalistic escapades over the years, Jeff Kamen, laboriously checked the text for accuracy (although, of course, any errors are my responsibility), making use of his intimate knowledge of military affairs. My tea-drinking pal, Steve Savage, provided crucial introductions to sources, as did my nephew, the journalist Hugh Eakin. Katrina Rill, the *Mother Jones Radio* producer, made interviews from that show available to me. Thanks to photographer Bob Fitch for the image of Robert Zabala.

Again, I enjoyed the enthusiasm of my radio partner Peter Morris, an early and vibrant supporter of the project. Don Wallenberg and Shawn Titen at MacNetworks in Santa Rosa, California, saved the work in progress when my iBook crashed. Kathy at DJ Word Processing in Santa Rosa did her usual expert job of transcribing what were often noisy interview tapes.

I must thank my friends Amy and Tom Valens for introducing me to Chelsea Green Publishing, an amazing independent publishing house. Publisher Margo Baldwin and editors John Barstow and Safir Ahmed are doing extraordinarily important work during these extraordinarily problematic times in which we live; check out the Chelsea Green catalog for scores of examples.

The practice of playing soccer using a foe's head for the ball – which Joshua Key described witnessing in Iraq – is not without precedent in the region, as difficult as such a scene may be to consider. Orphan Pamuk, in his memoir *Istanbul*, cites the illustrated *Istanbul Encyclopedia* reference to the decapitation of fifteenth-century Ottoman ruler Kara Mehmet Pasha. Pamuk questions, "Did the men really do as they did in the illustration and play soccer with the pasha's head?" Joshua Key's answer is yes.

Finally, I want to thank my classmate at American University, Pat Mackley. We did midcareer graduate work together and often talked about collaborating on a book about the Vietnam War from our two perspectives: his as a veteran who came back home to work against the war, mine as a stateside resister. But we lost track of each other over the years. I've thought of him often while working on *Mission Rejected*, and hope this book helps me find him again.

RESOURCES

Veterans for Peace identifies itself as an organization of "veterans working together for peace and justice through non-violence," and calls on its members to wage peace. They can be reached in St. Louis, Missouri, at (314) 725-6005 or www.veteransforpeace.org.

Iraq Veterans Against the War is organizing returning troops and soldiers still in Iraq who oppose the war. Their mission statement: "We are committed to saving lives and ending the violence in Iraq by an immediate withdrawal of all occupying forces. We also believe that the governments that sponsored these wars are indebted to the men and women who were forced to fight them and must give their Soldiers, Marines, Sailors, and Airmen the benefits that are owed to them upon their return home." They can be reached at www.ivaw.net and (215) 241-7123.

Veterans Against the Iraq War is a coalition of veterans from prior U.S. wars. Their website is www.vaiw.org and their telephone number is (201) 876-0430.

The GI Rights Hotline has a twenty-four-hour telephone number: (800) 394-9544. Their website is http://girights.objector.org.

Military Counseling Network is headquartered in Germany and offers soldiers on duty there services similar to those provided by the GI Rights Hotline. Their website is www.getting-out.de. Their phone number in Germany is 06223-47506.

National Center for Post-Traumatic Stress Disorder provides information about PTSD and its treatments on their web page at http://www.ncptsd.va.gov/faq.html.

The Central Committee for Conscientious Objectors "supports and promotes individual and collective resistance to war and preparations for war." Founded in 1948, it was a critical source of advice and guidance for men eligible for the draft during the Vietnam War and serves the same role for soldiers in today's volunteer army. The CCCO website is www.objector.org; it is headquartered in Oakland, at (510) 465-1617, and Philadelphia, at (215) 563-8787.

Military Families Speak Out is an "organization of people who are opposed to war in Iraq and who have relatives or loved ones in the military." The website is www.mfso.org and they can be reached by phone at (617) 983-0710.

Gold Star Families for Peace was founded by families whose relatives died as a result of the Iraq War. Their website is www.gsfp.org and their phone number is (562) 500-9079.

Bring Them Home Now uses the slogan, "Bush says bring 'em on, but we say bring them home now." Its members are veterans, military families, and active duty soldiers, and they can be reached through Veterans for Peace. Their website is www.bringthemhomenow.org.

Vietnam Veterans Against the War provides moral support and guidance to Iraq War veterans. Their web address is www.vvaw.org and their Chicago main office can be reached at (773) 276-4189. A corollary organization is the **Vietnam Veterans of America Foundation,** available at www.vvaf.org.

The National Lawyers Guild Military Law Task Force "assists those working on military law issues as well as military law counselors working directly with GIs." The web address is www.nlg.org/mltf and the phone number is (415) 566-3732.

Peace-Out offers detailed information for those interested in conscientious objector status. It maintains a database at its website of veterans who succeeded in obtaining CO discharges and who offer to counsel soldiers considering a CO route out of the service. That site is www.peace-out.com.

Conscientious Objector is a registry that offers soldiers an opportunity to use their depository to document the development of a conscientious objector mentality. Their web address is www.objector.us.

Traveling Soldier (www.traveling-soldier.org), **GI Special** (www.militaryproject.org), and **Truthout** (www.truthout.org) are online newsletters offering Iraq War news reports from an antiwar perspective. **Citizen Solider** (www.citizen-soldier.org) is a resource for books and videos about soldiers resisting war.

No More Victims is an organization founded to help Iraqi children injured as a result of the war. "We believe one of the most effective means of combating militarism is to focus on direct relief to its victims." Contact them at www.nomorevictims.org.

September 11th Families for Peaceful Tomorrows was founded by families of those killed in the 9/11 attacks who have "united to turn our grief into action for peace. By developing and advocating nonviolent options and actions in the pursuit of justice, we hope to break the cycles of violence engendered by war and terrorism." Find them at www.peacefultomorrows.org and (212) 598-0970.

United for Peace & Justice is a coalition of more than 1,300 activist groups throughout the United States who "protest the immoral and disastrous Iraq War and oppose our government's policy of permanent warfare and empire-building." Their address on the web is www.unitedforpeace.org, and their phone number is (212) 868-5545.

NOTES

1. Richard Keene's experiences were documented by Joseph Besse in his 1753 work *A Collection of the Sufferings of the People called Quakers, for the Testimony of a Good Conscience.*
2. http://www.pbs.org/itvs/thegoodwar/american_pacifism.html.
3. Dan Felushko made his "Died deluded in Iraq" comments to CBS reporter Scott Pelley for the program *60 Minutes Wednesday,* December 8, 2004.
4. Ibid.
5. "You Can't Wash Your Hands When They're Covered With Blood," Hart Viges, the *Independent* (London), September 24, 2005.
6. Cited at www.freecamilo.org.
7. "Will War Deserters Find Asylum in Canada?" Yochi J. Dreazen, the *Wall Street Journal*, February 8, 2006.
8. "They Can't Throw Us All in Jail," Geov Parrish, WorkingforChange.com, January 27, 2005.
9. In his speech to rally the troops at the Naval Academy, November 30, 2005.
10. "L.A. Times Bans 'Resistance Fighters' in Iraq News," Reuters dispatch, November 5, 2003.
11. Ibid.
12. Station CJOB, Winnipeg, June 10, 2005.
13. "Combat Duty in Iraq and Afghanistan, Mental Health Problems, and Barriers to Care," Charles Hooge et al, *New England Journal of Medicine*, July 1, 2004.
14. The Vietnam War veteran was interviewed for the NBC News documentary "Healing the Wounds," reported and produced by Peter Laufer, 1984.

15. Crystal is correct. In response to an Associated Press request under the Freedom of Information Act, the Pentagon in early 2006 released figures acknowledging a significant increase in the number of enlisted soldiers leaving the military. One factor cited: excessive weight.

16. From the book *Northern Passage: American Vietnam War Resisters in Canada*, by John Hagan, an author with further credits as a draft dodger and professor of law and sociology at Northwestern University and the University of Toronto. It was published by Harvard University Press in 2001.

17. Point 121 of the Immigration and Refugee Board decision. The full text can be seen at the Board's website explaining its decision: http://www.irb-cisr.gc.ca/en/decisions/public/hinzman/hinzman_e.htm#conclusion.

18. "American Deserters Find a Mixed Reception in Canada," Doug Struck, *Washington Post*, October 11, 2004.

19. Jeremy Hinzman's perspectives on his decision are recorded in detail on his website, www.jeremyhinzman.net. The site is packed with letters from supporters worldwide.

20. The UN Nuremberg principles can be read at http://untreaty.un.org/ilc/texts/instruments/english/draft%20articles/7_1_1950.pdf.

21. Carolyn Eagan, the president of the Toronto Council of the United Steelworkers, immigrated as a war resister with her husband during the Vietnam War.

22. "Stop-loss" orders force soldiers to remain in the military even though the time period of their volunteer commitment to the service is expired and they are due to be discharged. The Pentagon first issued stop-loss orders for the so-called War on Terror in November 2002. The stop-loss authority was first granted to the military by Congress in response to concerns about inadequate troop strength in the Vietnam War era.

23. Private Eddie Slovik was executed in 1945 for desertion, as ordered by General Dwight D. Eisenhower in an attempt to deter others. Over twenty thousand U.S. soldiers were convicted of desertion during World War II, but only Slovik was executed.

24. Among those working to draw attention to the requirement that schools give student contact information to the military is the organization Leave My Child Alone. It offers details in English and Spanish on how to opt out of the law's intrusion on students' personal lives and can be contacted at http://www.leavemychildalone.org.

25. "Military Recruiters Targeting Minority Teens," Erika Hayasaki, *Los Angeles Times*, April 5, 2005.

26. "For Recruiters, a Hard Toll From a Hard Sell," Damien Cave, *New York Times*, March 27, 2005.

27. Dubs are fancy chrome wheels.

28. "I am the Army."

29. Enlistment/Reenlistment Document, Armed Forces of the United States, page 2, DD form 4/1, January 2001. The uppercase letters are in the contract.

30. *Talk of the Bay*, radio station KUSP, Santa Cruz, California, May 24, 2005.

31. CBS News broadcast an extensive report documenting the abuses on May 20, 2005.

32. "Hardball Recruiter Gets Promoted," Lee Cowan, CBS.com, July 14, 2005.

33. "Sign Here, Kid," Mike Ferner, *The Objector*, January 2005, page 14.

34. *Democracy Now* radio program, interview by Amy Goodman, May 24, 2004.

35. "Breaking Ranks," David Goodman, *Mother Jones* magazine, November/December 2004.

36. *Kill! Kill! Kill!* by Jimmy Massey with Natasha Saulnier is published by Editions de Panama, Paris.

37. "Former Marine Testifies to Atrocities in Iraq," Doug Struck, *Washington Post*, December 8, 2004.

38. "5 in Iraq Family Die Near Busy U.S. base," Richard Boudreaux, *Los Angeles Times*, November 22, 2005.

39. The Army recruiting numbers were reported by Reuters and published in the September 13, 2005, *New York Times* article "Army Expects to Miss Goals for Recruiting."
40. "For Recruiters, a Hard Toll From a Hard Sell," Damien Cave, *New York Times,* March 27, 2005. Cave quotes Army statistics to get the AWOL recruiters total.
41. "Uncle Sam Wants You – Even If You're 42 Years Old," Rick Maze, *Army Times,* July 19, 2005.
42. The *Nation* obtained a copy of the Army's *School Recruiting Program Handbook*, and these quotes from it appeared in the magazine's article "Military Recruiters Are Now Targeting Sixth Graders. Who's Next?" by Karen Houppert, September 12, 2005.
43. Jim Murphy spoke in a Mother Jones Radio interview with Angie Coiro, broadcast on Air America Radio affiliates on September 11, 2005.
44. "Madison Avenue Wants You," Timothy O'Brien, *New York Times*, September 25, 2005.
45. Ibid.
46. Robert Koehler writes for and is an editor at the *Chicago Tribune*–owned Tribune Media Services; this column ran in the *San Francisco Chronicle* on August 18, 2005.
47. Bischel was a guest on "The Military Family in Crisis" edition of the LinkTV show called *FAQs,* October 27, 2004.
48. The Beetle Bailey strip is distributed by King Features Syndicate. The "alternatives to war" strip ran in the *International Herald Tribune* on October 15, 2005.
49. "Pentagon Estimates Iraqi Deaths," *Los Angeles Times*, October 30, 2005.
50. The methodology and background of Iraq Body Count, along with an updated tally, can be seen at www.iraqbodycount.net.
51. "Mortality Before and After the 2003 Invasion of Iraq: Cluster Sample Survey," Les Roberts, *The Lancet*, November 20, 2004.

52. "Why Numbers Matter," Marla Ruzicka, AlterNet.org, April 20, 2005.

53. "Soldiers' Gravestones Include Pentagon Operation Names," David Pace in an Associated Press dispatch printed in the Santa Rosa (California) *Press Democrat*, August 24, 2005.

54. Hagel made the "We're not winning" comments on the ABC program *This Week*, August 21, 2005.

55. General Odom made the remarks on September 28, 2005, at a news conference called by North Carolina Republican Congressman Walter Jones, who was introducing a House of Representatives resolution calling on President Bush to set a timetable for the withdrawal of U.S. armed forces from Iraq.

56. The Zinn interview was conducted for *Penthouse* magazine and appeared in issue 4 in 2004.

57. "Veteran of Iraq, Running in Ohio, Is Harsh on Bush," James Dao, *New York Times*, July 27, 2005.

58. "The Democrat Who Fought," David Goodman, *Mother Jones*, November 2005.

59. From the "War in Iraq" page of the Hackett for Congress website: www.hackettforcongress.com.

60. Congressman John Murtha's entire statement calling for an immediate pullout of U.S. forces from Iraq is posted on his website: http://www.house.gov/apps/list/press/pa12_murtha/pr051117iraq.html

61. Vice President Cheney's entire speech to the Frontiers of Freedom Institute, including his direct insults of Senators Harry Reid, John Kerry, and Jay Rockefeller, can be read at this page on the vice president's website: http://www.whitehouse.gov/news/releases/2005/11/20051116-10.html.

62. "Rapid Pullout from Iraq Urged by Key Democrat," Eric Schmitt, *New York Times*, November 18, 2005.

63. From David Cline's open letter to Congress, March 19, 2005. The full text is available at www.veteransforpeace.org.

64. The full text of President Bush's June 28, 2005, speech at Fort Bragg can be read at http://www.whitehouse. gov/news/releases/2005/06/20050628-7.html.
65. The blog was called "Fight to Survive" and can be seen at http://www.ftssoldier.blogspot.com.
66. The number at the USADIP to call to confirm deserter status is (502) 626-3711.
67. But note that cell phones that are switched on can be located with some precision even when calls are not made, and developing technology is allowing phone companies to locate callers more precisely.
68. From "Odyssey of Conscience: From Civilian CO to Cambodia," an autobiographical profile written by Morse in an undated fiftieth anniversary issue of the Central Committee for Conscientious Objectors magazine, *The Objector*.
69. At the sgtted.blogspot.com website, the writer only identifies himself as SGT Ted from California, "a 42 year old father, grandfather, soldier, piper, part-time rake and hellraiser."
70. *I Am a Soldier, Too: The Jessica Lynch Story*, by Rick Bragg, Knopf, 2003.
71. "Family Demands the Truth," Robert Collier, *San Francisco Chronicle*, September 25, 2005.
72. "Former Soldier Speaks Out Against the War in Iraq," Sandra Gonzales, *San Jose Mercury News*, May 2, 2005.
73. "Army Soldier Who Refused Iraq Duty Was Confused About Deployment, Attorney Says," Associated Press dispatch by Russ Bynum.
74. Details of the Amnesty International action in support of Kevin Benderman can be seen at http://web.amnesty. org/library/index/ENGAMR511372005?open&of =ENG-USA.
75. Kevin Benderman's letters from Fort Lewis can be read at http://www.topia.net/kbfortlewis.html.

76. " 'They Can't Train You for the Reality of Iraq. You Can't Have a Mass Grave with Dogs Eating the People in It.' Two Years After the War Began, A Growing Number of US Troops Are Refusing to Return to Iraq," Suzanne Goldenberg, the *Guardian* (London), March 19, 2005.
77. "Army Convicts Antiwar Iraq Veteran Blake LeMoine of Refusing Orders," Andy Buerger, Reuters, March 28, 2005.
78. LeMoine's "roach motel" analogy was quoted by the antiwar organization Refusing to Kill at http://www.refusingtokill.net/ USGulfWar2/BlakeLeMoine.htm.
79. "Few but Organized, Iraq Veterans Turn War Critics," Neela Banerjee, *New York Times*, January 1, 2005.
80. "A U.S. Soldier in Iraq Wonders: 'How Many More Must Die?'" Tim Predmore, *Peoria Journal Star*, August 24, 2003.
81. "Solider Killed in Iraq Opposed War but Tried to 'Do Some Good,'" *Denver Post*, November 19, 2005.
82. "Un-volunteering: Troops Improvise to Find a Way Out," Monica Davey, *New York Times*, March 18, 2005.
83. From an Associated Press dispatch, 2005.
84. "An Objection of Conscience," an essay by Jim Taylor, from the book *Shock and Awe: Responses to War*, Creative Arts Book Company, Berkeley, edited by Peter Laufer.
85. Stephen Funk's stand against the military was supported by the Resource Center for Nonviolence, which posted his statement on its website at http://www.rcnv.org/rcnv/archives/2003/sfunk.htm.
86. Stephen Funk's entire e-mail is posted at http://pages.prodigy.net/gmoses/nvusa/funk001.htm.
87. General John Abizaid was CENTCOM's commander-in-chief while Clifton Hicks served in Iraq.

INDEX